Physical Education

For CCEA GCSE

Derek Prentice

© Derek Prentice and Colourpoint Books 2006

ISBN: 978 1904242 59 8

First edition
Second impression

Layout and design: Colourpoint Books
Cover design: Malcolm Johnston
Printed by: W&G Baird Ltd

Colourpoint Books

Colourpoint House
Jubilee Business Park
21 Jubilee Road
Newtownards
Co Down
BT23 4YH

Tel: 028 9182 0505
Fax: 028 9182 1900
E-mail: info@colourpoint.co.uk
Web-site: www.colourpoint.co.uk

DEREK PRENTICE has over 30 years' experience of teaching Physical Education. Along with a small number of other PE teachers, he introduced examination Physical Education into Northern Ireland, and since then has continued to be involved in its development. He has been Chief Examiner for the subject for over 20 years, and has been part of the moderating team that visits schools. He is currently Vice Principal at Dundonald High School. He has written this textbook to help all students studying GCSE Physical Education.

He dedicates the book to his daughter Zahra who is a keen sportsperson.

Picture credits:
Cover image: Jupiter Images, www.comstock.com
IStockphoto*: 4, 5, 8 (bottom), 27, 35, 38 (middle & bottom), 39 (middle), 47, 49 (top), 51, 53, 54 (top), 55, 58, 61 (top), 64, 65, 83 (top), 84 (bottom), 86, 88 (top), 94 (bottom), 102, 104, 106, 109, 110, 111, 112, 114 (bottom), 115, 117 (bottom), 118, 119 (top), 120 (top), 123, 124 (bottom), 126, 127, 129, 130, 131, 134, 135, 137, 139 (top), 167
Marinela Sotonic: 6 (top)
Dan Colcer: 6 (climber)
Liina Viil: 6 (girl sleeping)
Peter Jancarik: 6 (two girls)
Adam Sablich (adam@slickware.com: 7 (top)
Getty Images**: 7 (bottom 3), 8 (top right), 79, 87, 93 (bottom right), 94 (top right), 116
Curtis Fletcher: 8 (top left)
Sergio Guidaux Kalil: 9
Melanie Kuipers: 10 (top)
Martin Walls: 10 (bottom), 11 (top)
Barbara Pastorini: 11, 13 &16 (potatoes)
Andre Lube: 11, 13 & 16 (bread)
Patrick Herman: 11 (sugar)
Matthew David Trow: 11 (butter)
Mario Carangi: 11 (meat)
Montse Teixidó: 11 (olive oil), 92 (golf)
Mark Csabai: 11 (eggs)
Ali Kerem Yucel: 11 (fish)
João Estêvão: 11 (peas), 22 (top)
George Georgiades: 12 (top), 18 (apple)
Bethan Hazell: 12 (middle)
Crissy Watkins: 12 (bottom)
Jo Jo Studio: 17 (top)
Hannah Gleghorn: 18 & 89 (pills)
Adam Ciesielski: 20, 21
Bülent İnce: 24

Georgios MW: 25 (top)
Renea Leathers: 25 (bottom)
Ames Goodwin: 26
Blazej Pieczynski: 31 (top)
Paul Chessare: 31 (bottom), 113 (bottom)
Derek Prentice: 33 (top & bottom), 40 (right), 48, 54 (bottom), 63, 89 (bottom), 94 (top left), 97 (bottom), 98, 101 (bottom), 105, 120 (middle), 128, 133
Lauren Lankford & ReflectedClarity Designs: 36 (bottom)
Matthias Schimmelpfennig: 37
Robert Alchinger: 38 (top)
Joana Franca: 66 (top)
Mario A Magallanes Trejo: 92 (top)
Carlo San: 92 (bottom)
Michal Koralewski: 93 (bottom left)
Paul Pasieczny: 99
Frederic Carmel: 113 (top)
Empics/TopFoto.co.uk: 117 (top)
Jørgen Zachariassen: 119 (bottom)
Brad Harrison: 120 (bottom)
Lotus Head: 121 (top)
Magda Skale: 121 (bottom)
Matt Williams: 124 (top)
Sarp Sencer: 144

*   Please see alongside individual images for photographers' member names.
** Please see alongside individual images for photographers' names.

All copyright has been acknowledged to the best of our ability. We apologise for any inadvertent omissions, which we shall endeavour to correct in any future edition.

Contents

* In the CCEA Specification, skilled performance is incorporated into each section. However, in order to make this book as user-friendly as possible, all the material relating to skilled performance has been gathered together into a discrete section.

Introduction

The main purpose of this book is to help you succeed at CCEA GCSE Physical Education.

The course requires you to think critically, to analyse, to evaluate, to plan, to apply, and to be creative with regard to physical health/wellbeing, peak physical fitness, and skilled performance.

This book provides you with the information and tools to be able to do this.

The CCEA course is divided into three components (parts).

○ Component 1: Terminal examination (30% of total marks)

Component 1 is assessed by one written examination paper of 1 hour and 30 minutes.

Area of study a: Factors affecting participation in physical activity

Section A of the examination paper will require you to answer questions on the facts, concepts, terminology, principles and methods needed to be able to do the planning, analysing and evaluating required for Section B.

Area of study b: Developing physical health/wellbeing, peak physical fitness, and skilful performance

Section B of the examination paper will require you to be able to plan effective exercise/training sessions and programmes for a range of individuals and their circumstances. It also will require you to be able to analyse, interpret and evaluate the safety, appropriateness and effectiveness of exercise/ training sessions and programmes for a range of individuals and their circumstances. These sessions or programmes will focus on physical health, physical fitness or skill.

◯ Component 2 : Individual performance in the physical activities (50% of total marks)

The facts, concepts, terminology, principles and methods that you will learn in this book can be applied to improve your physical fitness and skills in your selected physical activities.

◯ Component 3: Analysis and improvement of performance in your own exercise profile (20% of total marks)

What you learn in this book will also help you to effectively analyse and improve your own exercise profile.

This book will cover what you need to know, understand and be able to do in preparation for the oral examination.

You will want to learn not only from the information provided in these pages, but also from your own independent research using other resources and from your own practical experience. You need to think critically about information you encounter, be able to understand principles, and be capable of applying these principles creatively for yourself and for others.

To help you develop these skills, relevant tasks have been set in each of the book's 14 sections.

Section 1
Concepts

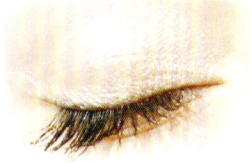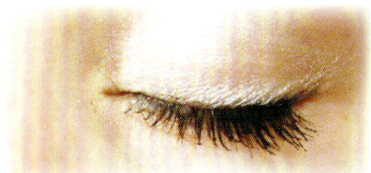

The concepts of health, fitness, and performance and the relationship between them

 **Health**

> The World Health Organization (WHO) defined health as "a state of complete physical, social and mental well-being and not merely the absence of disease or infirmity."
>
> *Preamble to the Constitution of the World Health Organization, 1946*

To be healthy means that you should be in good physical shape – a state of **complete physical wellbeing**. It is about looking after your body and doing the right things to keep it in good working order so that you can cope with the demands of everyday life, for example climbing stairs.

This means that you need to exercise regularly, eat the right kinds and amounts of foods, and avoid things that abuse the body, like smoking cigarettes.

If you don't keep your body in good working order it can lead to poor health and possibly disease or illness such as heart disease.

To be healthy also means that you should be mentally alert, happy, and be in control – a state of **complete mental wellbeing**. It is about looking after your brain and doing the right things to keep it in good working order so that you can cope with the demands of everyday life, for example GCSE examinations.

This means exercising your brain but also providing it with sufficient rest.

If you don't look after the brain it can lead to poor health and possibly disease or illness such as stress or depression.

To be healthy also means that you should be able to maintain good working relationships with others and good relationships with family and friends – a state of **complete social wellbeing**. It is about caring for others and behaving in an appropriate way with them, for example being courteous.

This means mixing and communicating, working with others, and exercising desirable social skills.

If you don't look after relationships with others it can lead to poor health and possibly illness such as stress or depression.

In summary, good health is more than the absence of disease and infirmity.

Good health involves the physical, mental, and social sides of our lives.

To maintain good health means doing positive things that promote good health and dealing with negative things that can harm our health.

The CCEA Specification focuses on physical health and wellbeing.

Physical fitness

Physical fitness is the ability to perform physical tasks efficiently and effectively.

Therefore, whether you are physically fit or not depends on the physical task you are set. Physical fitness is a relative concept. You can be fit for one task yet not be fit for another. It will depend on the type and level of fitness required for the task.

For example, a top athlete could be physically fit to win a gold medal at putting the shot in athletics because the task requires strength, but be unfit to run a 10,000m track race because the task requires endurance. You could be fit to play a full game as a goalkeeper but unfit to play a full game as a midfield player.

Stu Forster/Getty Images

Jamie Squire/Getty Images

Tony Duffy/Getty Images

Fit for what?

To find out if a person is physically fit you must ask "Fit for what?" or "What type of fitness and what level of fitness is required for the physical task or goal?" This definition covers physical fitness from the minimum of exercise needed to maintain physical health to performing at one's upper limit or potential to break a world record.

The difference between physical health and physical fitness

To maintain physical health you need to do appropriate and sufficient exercise/activity to keep your body in reasonable working order. This would be your baseline or benchmark. If you do less exercise than this it could lead to poor health.

To be physically fit you want to go above this baseline or benchmark. You want your body to be in better shape than normal so you do more exercise/training. Ultimately you want to exercise/train so that your body is in the best shape possible to perform your physical task or challenge as efficiently and effectively as possible.

This is **peak physical fitness**. If you go beyond this and do too much training it could lead to poor health.

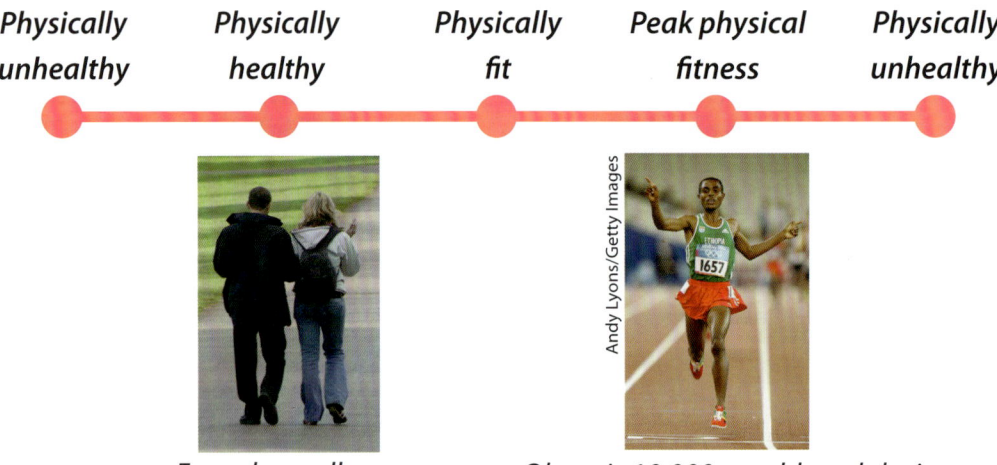

| Physically unhealthy | Physically healthy | Physically fit | Peak physical fitness | Physically unhealthy |

Everyday walkers   *Olympic 10,000m gold medal winner*

Exercise and training

When the term **exercise** is used, it refers to developing physical health/wellbeing. When the term **training** is used, it refers to developing peak physical fitness.

⭕ Skilled performance ▬▬▬▬▬▬▬▬

> Sparrow and Newell (1998) defined skill as "the ability to economically coordinate and control the movement to achieve the task goal."

Skilled performance or "skill" is the learnt ability to bring about a predetermined goal or result with maximum certainty and efficiency.

In physical education and sport we are often concerned with how well a task or performance is done.

⭕ SUMMARY

Section 1 has covered what you need to know and understand about the concepts of health, physical fitness and skilled performance (see Section 10 for more information on skilled performance). There are similarities and differences between the concepts.

Health includes basic physical fitness, but also includes mental and social wellbeing. Physical fitness goes beyond the normal fitness for health and prepares the body to perform to its potential for specific physical tasks. Physical fitness can be affected by health. Physical tasks can be purely physical or can involve skill. Learning is required when skill is involved. Skilled performance can be affected by the level of physical fitness.

Knowing and understanding the concepts is only the start. Ultimately, the CCEA GCSE course requires you to be able to:

- plan sessions and programmes of appropriate and sufficient exercise to gain or maintain physical health for a range of individuals and their circumstances
- analyse and evaluate the safety, appropriateness and effectiveness of given sessions or programmes
- plan training sessions and programmes to develop physical fitness for a range of athletes for specific events
- analyse and evaluate the safety , appropriateness and effectiveness of given sessions or programmes.
- plan skill-related workouts to develop skilled performance in sport
- analyse and evaluate the safety, appropriateness and effectiveness of given workouts

You will learn these skills later in the book.

▷ TASK on Concepts

Purpose

To help you think critically about definitions of the concepts and search for principles underpinning the concepts.

Instructions

Research the internet, other books and magazines for definitions of health, physical fitness and skill.

Can you see similarities and differences between the definitions for each concept?

List the definitions you like best and explain why you prefer them compared to other definitions.

Section 2
Lifestyle

Factors from lifestyle that affect the development of physical health/wellbeing, peak physical fitness, and skilled performance

From your study of Section 1 you should understand the concepts of health, physical fitness and skill.

In Section 2 you will consider how certain factors from a person's lifestyle can affect physical health/wellbeing, peak physical fitness, and skilled performance.

The **lifestyle factors** we will focus on are:

- diet
- drugs
- tobacco
- alcohol
- rest/sleep
- exercise

Later in Section 8 you will consider how your age, gender, height, weight, body proportions, body type, ratio of fast twitch muscle fibres to slow twitch muscle fibres, vital capacity and stroke volume can all affect your physical health/wellbeing, peak physical fitness, and skilled performance.

These are **genetic type factors** over which you have limited control. However, you *do* have control over lifestyle factors. You make the decisions.

◯ Diet

Your diet is your particular **eating pattern**. It is the mixture of foods that you eat in the amounts that you actually eat them.

You need to eat food:

- to maintain life
- for growth and repair
- to provide substances to regulate the processes of the body
- to carry out all voluntary physical activity

Foods are composed of combinations of the following:

- carbohydrates
- fats
- proteins
- vitamins
- minerals
- dietary fibre
- water

Carbohydrates

Carbohydrates are the main source for energy production in the body.

They can be classified as **complex carbohydrates**, for example potatoes and foods that are made from cereals (wholemeal bread, porridge), or as **simple carbohydrates**, for example sugar, honey and jam. It is best to eat complex carbohydrates as these naturally contain more vitamins, minerals and dietary fibre.

55–60% of the food you eat should be carbohydrates.

Fats

Fats are a secondary source for energy production and are vital for normal tissue functioning. Fat is also an insulator and protects vital organs.

Fat can be classified as being **saturated fat**, for example lard, butter or the fat on meat; **polyunsaturated fat**, for example sunflower oil or corn oil; or **monounsaturated fat**, for example olive oil.

It is better to eat polyunsaturated or monounsaturated fat rather than saturated fat.

Fats should make up 25–30% of the food you eat. Of this no more than 10% should be saturated fats.

Proteins

Proteins are needed for growth and repair of the body.

Proteins can be classified as **animal protein**, for example meat, poultry, fish, milk, cheese and eggs; or **vegetable protein**, for example peas, beans and nuts.

10–15% of the food you eat should be proteins.

Vitamins

Vitamins are needed for the functioning of muscles and nerves, the growth of body tissue and the release of energy from food. For example, some of the B vitamins are involved in the release of energy from foods, vitamin C releases iron from food, and vitamin D helps with the absorption of calcium from food.

All vitamins required by the body will be contained in a balanced and varied diet.

Minerals

Minerals, for example calcium, give strength and rigidity to bones. They also assist in many vital body functions. For example, phosphorus assists in the production of ATP (adenosine triphosphate) – the fuel for the release of energy from food. Iron is involved with the use of oxygen and is found in the haemoglobin in the red blood cells. Sodium is found in all body fluids but especially in the blood, and is involved in maintaining the water balance of the body. Sodium has a complementary action with potassium in the functioning of muscle and nerve activity.

There are also other minerals that are needed in very, very small quantities. These are known as the trace elements. Examples are fluorine, iodine and zinc.

All minerals and trace elements required by the body will be contained in a balanced and varied diet.

Water

Water is the main medium for transporting **nutrients** (food), removing waste, and regulating body temperature.

Water is crucial to life. Without water or fluids, adults will die within a week. The body can lose vast amounts of water through sweating. It is therefore important that you drink plenty of water or other fluids every day and especially when you sweat.

Dietary fibre

Dietary fibre is the part of the food that cannot be digested.

It is essential in that it provides bulk to the faeces. This helps prevent constipation and other more serious conditions.

Foods high in dietary fibre are usually complex carbohydrate foods.

Energy needs

Energy is measured in **joules** (J). 1,000 joules equals 1 **kilojoule** (kJ). 4.2 kilojoules equals 1 **kilocalorie** (kcal).

The number of kilocalories you need depends on your **metabolism**. Your metabolism is the rate at which you process or burn up your food. If you have a high metabolic rate then you process your food quickly and efficiently. If you have a low metabolic rate then you process your food slowly and less efficiently. Given the same amount of food each week, you would be less likely to become overweight if you had a high metabolic rate rather than a low metabolic rate.

When you exercise your metabolic rate rises. This means that you burn more kilocalories. When you stop exercising your metabolic rate continues to remain high for a period of time. This means you continue to burn kilocalories at a faster rate even though you have stopped exercising. This is why exercise, combined with a sensible kilocalorie-controlled diet, is an effective way to lose weight (fat).

The number of kilocalories you need is also influenced by your age, body size, body composition, gender, physical activity levels, and the climate.

You need more kilocalories as a teenager in your growth spurt than you need as a senior citizen.

The bigger your body is then the more kilocalories you need to keep it going. Males are generally bigger than females, so this accounts for the difference in the number of kilocalories needed by each gender.

In cold climates more kilocalories are needed to generate heat to stay warm. This generation of heat would not be required in hot climates so your body would require less kilocalories. Physical activity requires energy.

The more physically active you are the more kilocalories you need. If you are not physically active then you require fewer kilocalories.

The amount of kilocalories needed per day is 2,500 for the average man and 2,000 for the average woman. If they are very active this could rise to 3,500 for a man and 3,000 for a woman.

Foods contain varying amounts of carbohydrate, fat and protein. Each of these nutrients can provide energy.

Fat contains twice as much energy as carbohydrate or protein, but carbohydrate is the most efficient fuel for the production of energy. The figures in the table below illustrate this.

Food	Energy (kcal/g)	O^2 required (litres/g)	kcal equivalent (kcal/l)
Carbohydrate	4.1	0.81	5.1
Fat	9.3	1.98	4.7
Protein	4.3	0.97	4.4

It takes more litres of oxygen per gram to release the energy from fat than from carbohydrate. Therefore, when you take both factors into account (the amount of energy in the nutrients and the amount of oxygen needed to release that energy), you get more energy per litre of oxygen from carbohydrate than from fat.

Characteristics of a balanced, healthy diet

As we have discovered, people have different energy needs. The challenge is to get the balance right between energy intake and energy expenditure.

If your energy intake equals your energy expenditure then your body weight will stay constant.

Intake: 2,500kcal

Expenditure: 2,500kcal

If your energy intake is greater than your energy expenditure then your body weight will increase.

Expenditure: 2,000kcal

Intake: 2,500kcal

If your energy intake is less than your energy expenditure then your body weight will decrease.

Intake: 2,500kcal

Expenditure: 3,000kcal

Another challenge is to get the balance right between the nutrients in the total energy intake, that is the right balance between the intake of carbohydrates, fats and proteins.

The recommendation is:

- Carbohydrates should form 55–60% of total energy requirements.
- Fats should form 25–30% of total energy requirements.
- Proteins should form 10–15% of total energy requirements.

In summary, to plan a healthy, balanced diet, which requires no weight reduction, you should:

- aim to match energy intake to energy expenditure
- ensure that the balance between the nutrients falls within the guidelines above
- eat complex carbohydrates rather than simple carbohydrates for energy and dietary fibre
- ensure that no more than 10% of energy intake is from saturated fat. The remaining 15–20% should be monounsaturated or polyunsaturated fat.
- eat small quantities of meat, fish or poultry, or a wide variety of vegetables, pulses or legumes for protein
- eat a wide variety of vegetables, fruit and low-fat dairy products to have sufficient vitamins, minerals and dietary fibre

There are thought to be five main food groups:

bread, other cereals and potatoes
fruit and vegetables
milk and dairy products
meat, fish and alternatives
foods containing fats and foods containing sugar

Over a week you should aim to eat a variety of foods from each of the food groups using the following as guidance:

- Eat plenty from the bread, cereals and potatoes group. Base each meal around this food group, choosing wholemeal products where possible.
- Eat plenty from the fruit and vegetables group. You should aim to have five portions per day.
- Eat moderate amounts from the milk and dairy products group, choosing low-fat products where possible.
- Eat moderate amounts from the meat, fish and alternatives group. Choose low-fat meats and try to grill, roast or microwave rather than fry. You should eat fish about twice a week.
- Eat limited amounts from the foods containing fats and foods containing sugar group.

You need to be able to apply all this guidance practically. In other words, what would be a healthy breakfast? What would be a healthy lunch? What would be a healthy dinner? What are healthy snacks? How do you get the balance right for a day or over a week?

Similarities and differences between diets for health and diets for peak physical fitness

The same principles for a healthy diet apply to sportspeople who want to be at peak physical fitness.

In other words, energy intake must match energy expenditure. As sportspeople use a lot more energy when they are training and competing, they need to eat more food during these periods.

Again, the balance between the nutrients should be based on the guidelines listed on the previous page.

Carbohydrates are the best source of energy, so sportspeople who are training and competing and using lots of energy need to eat plenty of foods high in carbohydrate. Complex carbohydrates are best, but because of the high energy expenditure by sportspeople in hard training they sometimes need to supplement their complex carbohydrate intake with simple carbohydrates, in order to meet their high energy intake needs. Sportspeople should eat carbohydrates as soon after their training as possible.

Sportspeople who are involved in endurance events may use various methods of carbohydrate loading in the lead-up to major events. For example, for a few days they may restrict their carbohydrate intake to lower or deplete their body of this source of energy; this is then followed by a number of days which lead up to the event when they eat lots and lots of carbohydrates. It is thought that once the body is depleted of carbohydrates for a short time it will overcompensate, taking in and storing more than normal next time it is fed lots of carbohydrates. This is then beneficial for the sportsperson.

Pre-event meals should be eaten at least three hours before the event and should be light and easily digested. A light carbohydrate meal of mostly bread, pasta or potatoes and vegetables is suitable.

Like anyone aiming for a healthy diet, sportspeople in training should ensure that no more than 10% of energy intake is from saturated fat. The remaining 15–20% of their fat intake should be monounsaturated or polyunsaturated fat. Pre-event meals should avoid foods high in fat.

Again, like anyone aiming for a healthy diet, sportspeople in training should eat small quantities of meat, fish or poultry, or a wide variety of vegetables, pulses or legumes for protein. However, sportspeople tend to eat more protein than the average person. Since protein is for growth and repair, some feel that a **high protein diet** (a diet that has possibly 25% of total energy requirements from protein) and taking protein supplements will help them. On the other hand, it is thought to be sufficient for sportspeople to follow the general guidelines of 10–15% of total energy intake from protein while aiming to be at the upper end of the range – any additional intake of protein will be of no further benefit for growth and repair.

Sportspeople should also eat a wide variety of vegetables, fruit and low-fat dairy products to have sufficient vitamins, minerals and dietary fibre. If they do this there is rarely a need for vitamin or mineral supplements.

Hydration can be maintained by drinking plenty of fluids up to 30 minutes before training or a major event. During training or the event a sportsperson should, if possible, continue to drink small quantities at regular intervals.

Characteristics and effects of unbalanced, unhealthy diets

As we have seen, if your energy intake is less than your energy expenditure then your body weight will decrease. If the difference is sensible and controlled for a period of time to allow a target weight to be achieved then it is acceptable and your health should not suffer. However, if there is an extreme difference or the difference continues indefinitely then there comes a point where your performance and health will suffer. Prolonged **negative energy balance** can lead to deficiency diseases, starvation or **anorexia nervosa**.

People who live with severe negative energy balance have insufficient energy for ordinary everyday activities and are often bedridden. They are unable to perform or participate in sports. Growth and repair and the functioning of their bodies are also affected. If the condition is not treated it can lead to death.

If your energy intake is greater than your energy expenditure then your body weight will increase. A **positive energy balance** over a prolonged period of time will lead to weight gain. If this weight gain is not checked and controlled it will lead to **obesity** and an increased risk of ill health.

Physical performances will also be affected. The lungs of people who are overweight have to work harder to supply oxygen to the increased body mass, and the thick pads of fat can also restrict breathing. The hearts of overweight people have to work harder to supply oxygen to the increased body mass, and their arteries often fur up making it harder for the heart to pump the blood – thus leading to high blood pressure. Overweight people have greater wear and tear on their joints which can lead to arthritis. The layers of fat can also restrict their range of movement, so they generally find exercise much more difficult and uncomfortable. A vicious circle can be set up as the more uncomfortable people feel, the less they wish to exercise.

When there is an unsatisfactory balance between the nutrients in a diet it can lead to ill health. For example, coronary heart disease, high blood pressure, strokes, gallstones and diabetes are associated with diets high in fat, salt and cholesterol. Bowel cancer, appendicitis, irritable colon, diverticular disease, constipation and haemorrhoids are associated with diets low in fibre. Tooth decay and diabetes are associated with a high sugar intake.

TASK on Diet

Purpose

To help you to be creative in applying the principles underpinning healthy diets.

Instructions

Compose a healthy breakfast, lunch and dinner. Provide a detailed description of what is taken and explain your choices.

Drugs

There are various types of drugs:

- drugs that are taken daily, for example caffeine in coffee
- drugs that can be bought legally over the counter, for example paracetamol
- drugs that have some restrictions on their use, for example tobacco and alcohol
- drugs that can only be prescribed by a doctor, for example antibiotic drugs
- drugs that are illegal but used socially, for example cocaine
- drugs that are used to enhance performance in sports, for example anabolic steroids

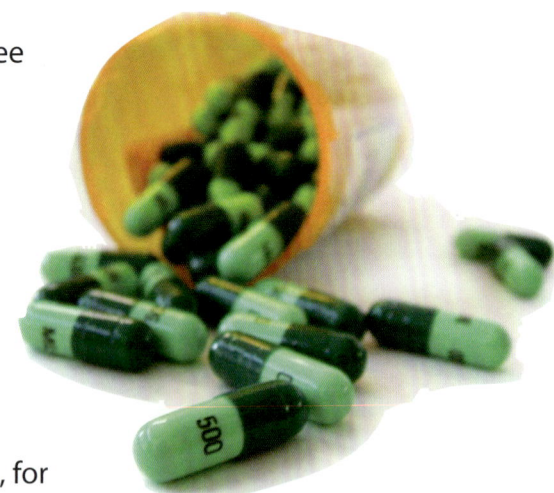

There are many illegal drugs that are forbidden by law, for example cannabis, heroin and cocaine. Many of the reasons they are banned are to do with health. People take these drugs for pleasure or self gratification. You may have already learnt about some of these illegal drugs in subjects such as Science, and Personal, Social and Health Education.

Our focus here will be on the immediate or short-term effects of various classes of drugs that enhance (improve) physical performance, and their long-term effects on health.

In one dictionary a drug is defined as "any synthetic or natural chemical substance used in the treatment, prevention, or diagnosis of disease" (Collins, 1986), yet we know drugs are used outside this context. In this wider context a drug could therefore be regarded as any synthetic or natural chemical substance that, when taken, alters the working of the mind or body.

Doping is a term used in sport. It can be defined as the use of those substances or methods which have been banned by relevant international and national sports governing bodies.

Should doping be banned from sport?

Some would argue that there should be no ban and that athletes should be able to take whatever drugs they want, or use whatever methods they want, to enhance or improve their performances. Doping would be fair as it would be open to everyone. Athletes should be able to decide whether they use drugs or not, as they are responsible for their own health.

On the other hand, if doping were allowed in sport it would mean chemists competing against each other to produce the most effective drugs or doping methods to improve performance. Athletes would be under pressure to take drugs as they would probably feel it was their only chance of success. Their health would be put at risk as the doses of many of the drugs can cause side effects. Doping would also set a bad example for children who wish to follow in the footsteps of their sporting heroes.

Sport should be characterised by the following values:

- open to all
- respect for rules and laws
- respect for self and other participants
- ethics, fair play and honesty
- promotion of health
- excellence in performance
- character and education
- fun and joy
- teamwork
- dedication and commitment
- courage
- community and solidarity

If you consider the values of sport, fair play, and the "spirit of sport", doping does not fit in. International and national sports governing bodies do not want doping to be allowed in sport.

These governing bodies decide the rules and laws for their sports, to promote fair competition and to protect the health of participants. If people wish to compete in a sport then they must be prepared to respect, accept and play by the rules, including the rules on doping.

The World Anti-Doping Agency (WADA) was established in 1999 to "promote and coordinate the fight against doping in sport internationally. WADA was set up as a foundation under the initiative of the IOC (International Olympic Committee), with the support and participation of intergovernmental organisations, governments, public authorities, and other public and private bodies fighting against doping in sport" (www.wada-ama.org).

Effect of drugs on health and physical performance

You should know the types of drugs that are banned, why sportspeople would want to use any of them illegally, and some side effects that can occur as a result of their use. Some of the drugs listed below, for example caffeine, are not banned altogether, but if the concentration in the body is above a certain limit it is considered doping.

Class of drugs	Why sportspeople use them	Potential harmful side effects
Stimulants *eg amphetamine, cocaine, caffeine, ephedrine* Stimulants can be found in cold and hay fever preparations. They stimulate the central nervous system.	To get the same effect as adrenalin; to get alertness, wakefulness and an increased ability to concentrate. Could be used by a wide range of sportspeople.	Addiction; high blood pressure (hypertension); palpitations and heart rhythm disorders; increased body temperature (hyperthermia); loss of appetite; loss of sleep (insomnia); restlessness, agitation, tenseness; hallucinations (psychosis); death
Narcotic analgesics *eg morphine, diamorphine (heroin), methadone* They act on the central nervous system to reduce feelings of pain.	To reduce or mask the feelings of pain; to depress coughs. Could be used by a wide range of sportspeople.	Addiction; nausea and vomiting; loss of sleep and depression; breathing becomes slower; decreased heart rate; constipation; loss of balance and coordination; decreased ability to concentrate.
Anabolic agents *eg anabolic steroids* They help build tissue by promoting the formation of protein in the skeletal muscles.	To increase muscle size and strength (to be effective the athlete needs to be doing strength training). More likely to be used by sportspeople competing in weightlifting, throwing and sports involving strength.	High blood pressure (hypertension); liver and kidney abnormalities; promotes growth of tumours. In males: breast development; infertility; diminished male hormone; prostrate cancer; hair loss. In females: male pattern hair growth and baldness; menstruation disturbances; decreased breast size; deeper voice.

Class of drugs	Why sportspeople use them	Potential harmful side effects
Diuretics They increase the rate of urine formation and excretion.	To try to achieve rapid weight loss. More likely to be used by sportspeople competing in sports where weight categories are involved, eg boxing, weightlifting and judo. In body building diuretics may be used to 'dry up' (to remove fluid) so muscles appear more defined. Could be used by any sportsperson to mask drug use by trying to reduce the concentration of drugs in the urine.	Dehydration; heart rhythm abnormalities (arrhythmias); decreased blood volume (hypovolemia); muscle cramps; dizziness when standing up (orthostatic hypotension); renal disorders.
Peptide hormones and analogues *eg growth hormone, insulin, EPO* These are natural or synthetic substances that act as messengers causing the production of other hormones.	To increase muscle size and strength (to be effective the athlete needs to be doing strength training); can reduce pain, repair damaged muscle and thus aid recovery. More likely to be used by sportspeople competing in weightlifting, throwing and sports involving strength. Erythropoietin or EPO would improve aerobic performances as it increases the number of red blood cells in the blood, and is more likely to be used by sportspeople competing in endurance events.	EPO: Increased viscosity (thickness) of the blood; high blood pressure (hypertension); blood clots; heart attack (myocardial infarction); stroke (cerebral infarction); convulsions.
Beta-blockers These are used to treat high blood pressure, angina, migraine, and cardiac arrhythmias.	To control anxiety; to steady and slow the heart rate; to reduce hand tremor. More likely to be used by sportspeople competing in sports like archery, shooting, and diving.	Cardiac failure; impaired circulation; low blood pressure (hypotension); slow heart rate (bradycardia); impotence; loss of sleep (insomnia).
Blood doping This means giving blood or related red blood products to an athlete.	To improve aerobic performance. More likely to be used by sportspeople competing in endurance events.	Blood clots; infections (hepatitis, AIDS) from donor blood or sharing needles; life-threatening hypersensitivity reaction (anaphylactic shock); allergic reactions (fever, rash).

Tobacco

Tobacco smoke contains over 4,000 chemicals, around 50 of which are known to cause cancer. The main components and most dangerous ones are:

nicotine

tar

carbon monoxide

Nicotine

Nicotine is a powerful, fast-acting drug that is very addictive, and smokers become dependent on it. It can affect the brain within ten seconds of being breathed in. Nicotine:

- constricts the blood vessels
- raises the heart rate
- raises blood pressure
- speeds up metabolism
- affects mood and behaviour
- combined with carbon monoxide, leads to clotting of the blood and clogging of the arteries

Tar

Tar is the sticky brown substance that carries many of the harmful substances into the lungs. It also stains smokers' fingers and teeth a yellowy-brown colour. Tar:

- carries irritants that narrow the bronchioles (small tubes) of the lungs
- carries irritants that irritate the delicate mucus membrane lining the air passages, causing them to produce more mucus
- carries irritants that damage the cilia (small hairs lining the air passages) that help protect the lungs from dirt and infection
- carries the carcinogens that can cause cancer

Carbon monoxide

Carbon monoxide is a poisonous gas. It:

- is taken up by the red blood cells which should normally be carrying oxygen

Effects of smoking on physical performance

Smoking constricts the lungs' air passages, making it more difficult to breathe air into the lungs. For a set work rate you would have to breathe faster and deeper than before to get the required amount of oxygen. Aerobic performance would therefore be less efficient.

The tar, dust and soot from the smoke lies in the alveoli (air sacs) in the lungs. This means there is less surface area than before for the exchange of oxygen and carbon dioxide. For a set work rate you would have to breathe faster and deeper than before to get the required amount of oxygen, again resulting in less efficient aerobic performance.

Due to blood vessels being constricted the heart has to work harder and blood pressure will be raised. For a set work rate the heart would have to beat faster than before to get the required amount of oxygen to the muscles, and aerobic performance would therefore be less efficient.

With carbon monoxide taking the place of oxygen in the red blood cells there is less oxygen available than before. For a set work rate the heart would have to beat faster than before to get the required amount of oxygen to the muscles, making aerobic performance less efficient.

To be able to work aerobically at a particular work rate the muscles demand a certain amount of oxygen per minute. If, due to smoking, less oxygen is getting into the lungs and less oxygen is taken into the blood from the lungs, then the respiratory (including the lungs) and the circulatory (including the heart) systems will have to work harder than before to meet the demand of the muscles. The tables below help illustrate this.

Performance as a non-smoker doing the 20m progressive shuttle-run test			
Lap	Heart rate (bpm – beats per minute)	Anaerobic threshold (bpm – beats per minute)	Comment
50	100	170	Heart has 70bpm in reserve.
70	130	170	Heart has 40bpm in reserve.
90	170	170	Heart crosses anaerobic threshold.
Stops due to fatigue at 94 laps			

Performance as a smoker doing the 20m progressive shuttle-run test			
Lap	Heart rate (bpm)	Anaerobic threshold (bpm)	Comment
50	130	170	Heart has 40bpm in reserve.
70	170	170	Heart crosses anaerobic threshold.
Stops due to fatigue at 73 laps			

As a result of these factors, a smoker will be at a disadvantage in aerobic activities.

Smoking can also affect learning ability and a number of reasoning tasks employed during test taking.

Long-term effects of smoking on health

No amount of smoking is free of risk. The amount of risk depends on how long you have smoked, how many you smoke, how deeply you inhale, and on genetic factors.

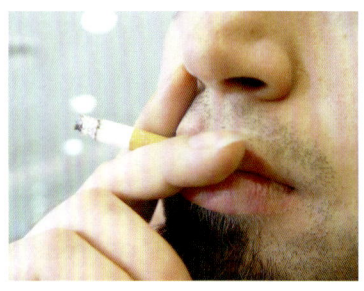

Some of the long-term effects of smoking are listed below:

Effects on respiratory system:

- Smokers have a much greater risk of getting lung cancer.
- Smokers have a much greater risk of getting mouth, nose and throat cancer.
- Smokers have a much greater risk of getting chronic bronchitis and emphysema.
- Colds, flu and laryngitis last much longer with those who smoke and smokers get more infections.

Effects on heart and circulation:

- Smokers have a much greater risk of a having heart attack.
- Smokers have a much greater risk of getting leukaemia.
- Smokers have a much greater risk of getting arteriosclerosis (build-up of fatty deposits and loss of elasticity in the artery walls). Arteriosclerosis is the forerunner to a range of diseases, for example strokes, and clotting of the blood in the legs.

Some other effects:

- Death. You must consider that you will have a shorter life expectancy as a smoker. It is said that each cigarette you smoke takes about 11 minutes off your life expectancy. Deaths due to smoking start from around the age of 35.
- Smoking accelerates premature ageing.
- Women who smoke reach menopause between one and three years earlier than non-smokers.
- Pregnant women who smoke make their babies smoke as well. Such babies are more likely to be born prematurely or underweight, and when they start walking may show signs of lack of coordination and general ill health.
- Smokers can become impotent and suffer adverse effects on fertility.
- Smoking can interfere with the healing of bone and muscle injuries.
- Smokers have bad breath, their hair and clothes smell, and their teeth and fingers become stained.
- Passive smoke affects the health of family and workmates.
- Smokers have a much greater risk of causing fires in their homes.
- Smokers are wasting their money.

⭕ Alcohol

Alcohol is a toxic drug. Drink too much of it at one time and it will poison you – you could go into a coma and you could even die. Drink too much of it over a prolonged period of time and your body cannot cope and your health suffers.

If, on the other hand, you consume alcohol in moderation, this allows the body time to cope with it and to make it safe by breaking it down and cleansing it from the body.

One unit of alcohol is 10ml. One unit is equivalent to half a pint of ordinary strength beer, one glass of wine, or one measure of spirits

The upper limit for 'low-risk drinking' is up to three units per day for men, and up to two units per day for women. It is *not* safe to consume a week's limit in one or two nights. Women have a lower limit than men mainly because women's bodies tend to be smaller, and have more fat and less water –this means that the alcohol is less diluted and stays in the body for longer.

Effects of alcohol on physical performance

Alcohol in small quantities, if it is legal in the rules of the particular sport, may help sportspeople in activities like darts, shooting or archery as it can relax the person, lower anxiety and reduce hand tremor.

In most sports, being under the influence of alcohol whilst competing would not be helpful as the effects of alcohol on the brain lead to:

- loss of coordination
- loss of balance
- poor information processing
- poor judgement and decision-making
- slowed reflexes/reaction time
- distorted vision
- slurred speech
- memory lapses
- blackouts
- nausea

Long-term effects of alcohol on health

Too much alcohol over a prolonged period of time can lead to:

- liver damage and disease. Your liver breaks down the alcohol in your blood. This is a slow process – one unit of alcohol per hour.

- cirrhosis of the liver

- increased risk of fertility problems

- obesity. Alcohol contains kilocalories but no essential nutrients like vitamins and minerals.

- depression. Alcohol is a depressant.

Researchers believe that alcohol taken in moderation may reduce the risk of heart disease.

Rest/Sleep

Rest is a period of time when you consciously try and get the mind and/or body to be inactive.

Sleep is a time of rest during which consciousness of the world is suspended.

Sleep is an essential component of health. Quality sleep promotes and maintains good health and physical performance. Sleep deprivation causes ill health and poor physical performances.

Rest/sleep and exercise/training work together – the benefits of exercise/training are optimised if your body gets adequate rest/sleep.

There are many factors that affect the quality of sleep. Two to consider are your **lifestyle** and your **environment**.

Lifestyle factors

- Diet – caffeine (contained in coffee, tea, cola, chocolate) is a stimulant and can prevent you from getting to sleep. Spicy and acidic foods or eating a big meal before you go to bed can cause heartburn and indigestion.

- Tobacco – nicotine is a stimulant and can prevent you from getting to sleep. Nicotine is also addictive and smokers tend to wake up after two to three hours of sleep due to nicotine withdrawal.

- Alcohol – this induces light sleep but impairs the deeper and more restorative stages of sleep.

- Drugs – many herbal supplements, over-the-counter or prescription medications activate the brain and cause sleep disruption.

- Exercise – exercise during the day can help you sleep but exercise just before you go to bed can prevent you from getting to sleep.

Environmental factors

Noise, light, extreme temperatures and changes in your environment can interfere with your sleep.

Effects of rest/sleep on physical performance and health

Sleep allows growth to occur. Human growth hormone is released under conditions of sleep. Sleep deprivation or poor-quality sleep can interfere with this and in the long term growth will be affected, which in turn can affect performances.

Sleep allows the repairing of muscles, neurons in the nervous system and other tissues, and the replenishing of immune cells. This repairing is maximal during sleep as energy consumption is lowered and is directed towards the healing or recovery process. Sleep deprivation or poor-quality sleep can interfere with this, the repair and recovery will not be as effective, and performances will therefore suffer.

Sleep allows the brain to recharge. Motivation is highest when mental alertness is highest. Performances are best when you are motivated and alert. Sleep deprivation or poor-quality sleep can affect alertness and motivation, causing performances to suffer.

©iStockphoto.com/DNY59

Sleep facilitates memory, learning and social processes. Sleep enables the brain to encode new information and store it properly. The parts of the brain that control emotions, decision-making and social interactions slow down during sleep, allowing optimal performance when awake.

Sleep follows a pattern and has a number of stages. To fully recover, your brain must experience all of these stages. If sleep deprivation or poor-quality sleep prevents this you will not be at your peak and therefore performances will suffer.

Sleep will be difficult in nights to come if you oversleep some days. Irregularity of sleep schedules can affect you and therefore your performances. You need to get the pattern right.

Sleep deprivation accumulates over time and can lead to decreased attentiveness and concentration, decreased short-term memory, poor coordination, delayed reaction times, poor decision-making, moodiness, irritability and anxiety. You can perform as badly as or worse than someone who is intoxicated (drunk).

Sleep deprivation over time can lead to depression.

Sleep interruption over time increases the risk of developing cancer.

Recent research suggests that sleeping with a light in the bedroom may increase the risk of cancer. Melatonin, a natural hormone our body produces by night which helps support the immune system and healing, is not produced to the same extent when light is present – thus affecting the immune system.

Your body knows when it needs rest. Learn to listen to it.

Sleep, rest and recovery allow the body to adapt to the stresses of training and this adaptation by your body is what makes you fitter than before. If athletes in hard training do not get sufficient sleep, rest or recovery from their training sessions, they will become overly fatigued and listless. Instead of becoming fitter they are more likely to be susceptible to colds and other illnesses and suffer from ill health.

Sleep, rest and recovery are therefore vital when exercising for physical health or training to achieve peak physical fitness.

TASK on Sleep

Purpose

To help you to develop your critical and creative thinking.

Instructions

From reading the section on sleep/rest, draw up a list of things that should be avoided or should not happen if you are to benefit fully from a good night's sleep.

Use the internet, books, magazines, leaflets and your understanding of the section to help you write this list.

Exercise

From Adam and Eve right up to the late 1800s human beings have had to depend on their own physical capabilities to build shelter, hunt for or gather food, fetch water, plant and harvest crops, look after animals, travel between places, and when necessary defend themselves against attack. Life was physical. Any work that was done required physical effort. Early machines helped ease the workload, but physical effort was still required.

Since the invention and development of the internal combustion engine (eg car engine) and the electric motor, machines now do most of the physical work in industry, agriculture and at home.

Consider a building site today compared to a few hundred years ago – today a man in a JCB digger would dig out the foundations whereas previously it would have been done by men with shovels.

Today a combine harvester can cut, thresh and bag crops as it is driven round a field, whereas in the past men would have had to cut the crop by hand, gather it by hand, thresh it by hand, and then bag it. Today an automatic washing machine washes your clothes and a tumble drier dries them, whereas this would once have been done manually.

Today, there are not as many physical jobs as there once were, heavy work in jobs is often restricted, and people are doing manual work less hours per day, week and year than ever before. Many people's jobs now involve sitting at a desk for most of the day so minimal physical effort is required.

If you consider people's lifestyles today you would find that many people drive to and from work or use public transport, they drive to and from the shops, and they sit and watch television or use a computer in their leisure time.

Because of the changes in work and the changes in lifestyle it has become necessary to plan sufficient and appropriate physical activity into people's lifestyles, in order to keep bodies healthy and in good working order.

The human body is built for use. The more it is used the more efficient it becomes. The less it is used the less efficient it becomes and the more likely it is to break down.

For example, with sufficient and appropriate exercise:

- **The respiratory system will work more efficiently**. You will be able to take in more air in each breath and over a minute.

- **The circulatory system will work more efficiently**. You will be able to deliver more blood to the working muscles with less effort.

- **The musculatory system will work more efficiently**. You will be able to produce more energy to keep you going at physical tasks and produce more strength and power for physical tasks.

There are also further benefits. For example, regular and appropriate exercise:

- **can help with weight control.** It helps burn up excess fats. If you stop exercising but continue to eat the same quantity of food as before you will put on weight.

- **can help with posture.** It tones the muscles so that you can keep your body in the positions that result in good posture. Lack of exercise means the muscles lose their tone and cannot maintain good posture, so you slouch and cannot stand up straight for any length of time.

- **can help with self-confidence.** The fit are more likely to sleep well, look well (shape and posture), feel good, and therefore be more confident in themselves. Lack of exercise can mean you become fat, lose your posture, feel unhappy about your shape, and feel that you can do very little – so you lose your self-confidence.

- **can help control negative habits** such as smoking, drugs, excessive eating and excessive intake of alcohol. When you are fit you are more concerned about and inclined to look after your body, and so not as likely to get involved in these negative habits.

- **can help with rest/sleep.** Exercise can make you physically tired and therefore help you to get to sleep at night. Lack of exercise can make you feel you haven't done anything and are not tired, so you will have difficulty getting to sleep.

- **can help reduce the risk of some illnesses and diseases.** If you are fit and healthy your body is in good working order, you are less at risk of suffering from a heart attack, angina or arteriosclerosis (build up of fatty deposits and loss of elasticity in the artery walls). You are also less likely to become obese or suffer from osteoporosis (brittle bones).

- **can help relieve stress.** A stressful day when everything seems to be on top of you can be turned around by a session of exercise. It can take your mind off the problems, give you a different perspective, and re-energise you. If you do not exercise you do not gain these benefits.

- **can help extend a healthy active life.** If you are fit and healthy your body is in good working order and therefore can continue to perform everyday tasks with ease. This makes you seem younger. If you don't exercise you lose your capability to perform everyday tasks and therefore may appear to be older than you are.

SUMMARY

In Section 1 you explored the concepts of health, peak physical fitness and skilled performance.

In Section 2 you have looked at factors that affect your physical health, peak physical fitness and skilled performance.

A state of physical wellbeing or peak physical fitness doesn't just happen. It depends on the decisions you make about your lifestyle and on the actions you take.

You decide whether you smoke cigarettes, drink alcohol or take illegal drugs, and then you act accordingly. If you know and understand the effects that they have on your health and performance it can help you make the right decisions.

In order to have a healthy lifestyle, you should choose never to smoke or take illegal drugs. With alcohol the decision is not quite so straightforward – you can have a healthy lifestyle by choosing not to drink at all (teetotal) or by choosing to drink only in moderation.

With sleep, diet and exercise it is not simply a "yes" or "no" decision. With sleep you have to know the amount and quality that you need for health, peak physical fitness and skilled performance, and how you can achieve the right balance.

With diet you need to know how much you should eat and what foods you should eat for health, peak physical fitness and skilled performance, and how you can achieve the right balance.

For exercise you need to know what exercise you should do, how hard you should exercise, how long you should exercise for, and how often you should exercise per week or month to promote physical health or peak physical fitness.

Sections 3 to 5 and 12 to 13 will focus on exercise/training and provide you with the information you need.

Section 3

Components

Components that affect the development of physical health/wellbeing and peak physical fitness

In Section 1 you learnt that physical fitness is a relative concept in that you can be fit for one physical task but not fit for another. That is because there are different types of fitness. You could be fit in one type of fitness and therefore perform well in physical tasks involving that type of fitness, and at the same time you could be unfit in another type of fitness and therefore perform less well in physical tasks involving that type of fitness.

Physical tasks can require the same type of physical fitness but demand different levels of that fitness. To achieve a qualifying time to run in the World Athletics Championships for the 10,000m track race requires a different level of physical fitness compared to that required to complete a 10km fun run.

⬤ Components of physical fitness

There are seven components of physical fitness. They are:

- aerobic energy production
- anaerobic energy production
- muscular power
- muscular strength
- muscular speed
- muscular endurance
- flexibility

You need to know and understand each of these components and what determines your physical fitness in each of them.

To perform any physical task you require energy. Energy can be produced **aerobically** or **anaerobically**.

Aerobic energy production

Aerobic energy is produced **with the use of oxygen.**

Aerobic energy production is determined by the ability of the respiratory and circulatory systems to deliver nutrients and oxygen to the working muscles and the ability of the working muscles to use the supply.

Aerobic fitness is about being able to keep going at activities such as running, cycling, swimming or rowing for long periods of time without getting tired.

Aerobic activities are activities in which the major muscles of the body are worked and in which the respiratory and circulatory systems can meet the energy demands of the activities.

Anaerobic energy production

Anaerobic energy is produced **without oxygen.**

Anaerobic energy production is determined by the ability of the muscles and liver to store fuel and the ability of the muscles to utilise this fuel.

Anaerobic fitness is about being able to perform at very high intensities or maximum effort.

Anaerobic activities can be those requiring very high-intensity efforts which last less than ten seconds, for example a short flat-out sprint, putting the shot, or throwing the hammer. They can also be activities where the respiratory and circulatory systems for a time cannot deliver sufficient nutrients and oxygen to the working muscles to allow them to work at the intensity required by the activity.

For example, a 400m sprint race or doing as many press-ups as possible in two minutes will involve the use of energy produced anaerobically. The body is capable of working at high intensities for a short period of time without needing oxygen. Fuel stored in the muscles and liver can be used to produce energy without the use of oxygen.

Muscles require energy to produce force for carrying out physical tasks. This energy is usually generated from a combination of aerobic and anaerobic energy. The force produced by the muscles can provide **power**, **strength**, **speed** or **endurance**.

Muscular power

Muscular power is about being able to produce maximum force, or a considerable force, with speed in an explosive effort.

Competition weightlifting is an activity that requires muscular power in that to overcome the resistance, maximum force is required in one explosive effort. Shot put and hammer throwing are also activities which require muscular power. In these activities the physical task requires less force but more speed.

Muscular power is determined by the ability of the muscle or group of muscles to produce force with speed in an explosive effort.

Muscular strength

Muscular strength is about being able to lift, push, pull or move heavy things easily.

Muscular strength activities are those such as tug-of-war or maintaining a push in a rugby scrum, as the muscles are required to produce a near maximum force over a short period of time.

Muscular strength is determined by the ability of a muscle or group of muscles to produce near maximum force over a short period of time.

Muscular speed

Muscular speed is about being able to apply a moderate to small force at high speed.

Playing shots in racket games such as badminton or tennis or strokes in games such as golf involve muscular speed, as the shots or strokes involve applying a moderate force at high speed.

Muscular speed is determined by the ability of a muscle or group of muscles to contract and relax quickly.

Muscular endurance

Muscular endurance is about being able to hold or to keep repeating a movement for a long period of time. The length of time will depend on the amount of force that the muscle, or group of muscles, is required to produce.

Holding two light dumbbells for as long as possible with your arms straight and your hands at shoulder height involves muscular endurance. Continually playing shots in badminton or tennis requires muscular endurance in the arms, wrists and fingers, and continually repeating cycling or running movements requires muscular endurance in the muscles of the legs.

Muscular endurance is determined by the ability of a muscle or group of muscles to work for long periods of time at less than maximum effort.

Flexibility

Flexibility is about being able to bend, stretch, twist and turn easily.

Being able to perform a high kick in dance, the splits in gymnastics or the butterfly with good technique in swimming requires flexibility.

Flexibility is determined by the ability of the muscles and ligaments surrounding joints to stretch to allow the full range of movement at the joints.

◯ Physical health/wellbeing

Energy production for physical health/wellbeing

When you consider the type of energy production needed for everyday life then aerobic energy production would rate as being very important and anaerobic energy production as not very important.

For example, the physical work or tasks done in most jobs (walking, climbing the stairs, etc) and during leisure time (gardening, decorating, etc) are nearly all aerobic-based. There are not many everyday activities that demand maximum or high-intensity efforts. It is only occasionally that you may need to sprint for a bus or to get out of the rain.

This means an exercise programme to develop or to maintain physical health/wellbeing should consist mostly of aerobic-based exercise.

Muscular fitness for physical health/wellbeing

When you consider the demands made for everyday life, muscular endurance and muscular strength would be important and muscular power and muscular speed would be of little importance.

Most of the time, things that need to be lifted, pushed, pulled or moved are only moderately heavy, for example shopping bags, saucepans, vacuum cleaners and lawn mowers. Since these actions take place over a time they require muscular endurance. There are also occasions when heavy things need to be lifted, pushed, pulled or moved, for example moving an armchair, pushing a car or lifting a bag of coal. These actions require muscular strength. There are not many everyday occasions that demand muscular power or muscular speed.

This means that an exercise programme to develop or to maintain physical health/wellbeing should contain exercises for improving muscular endurance and muscular strength.

Finally, many everyday tasks require you to bend, stretch, turn or twist, and flexibility therefore is very important. You need to be able to bend to tie your shoe laces or to pick something up from the floor; you need to be able to stretch to reach things from a high shelf; and you need to be able to twist your body and turn your head to see what is behind you.

This means that an exercise programme to develop or to maintain physical health/wellbeing should contain exercises for improving flexibility.

In summary, an exercise programme for physical health/wellbeing should contain a balance of aerobic exercise, and muscular exercises for endurance, for strength and for flexibility.

Physical fitness profiles
for events, sports and positions within sports

Many physical tasks involve all seven components of fitness to some extent. However, for most physical tasks, events, sports or positions within sports some components are more important than others.

Being able to decide the relative importance of the components of fitness for an event, sport or position within a sport is an important first step towards planning an appropriate and effective physical fitness training programme. This step helps you make the training specific or appropriate for the event, sport or position, and helps you decide the amount of time that should be spent on the various components.

In order to decide the relative importance of the components of fitness, you analyse the physical demands of the task, event, sport or position, then based on this analysis you rate the importance of the various components. If one component is very important then you will spend more time working on it than on one that is of little importance.

Physical demands of 100m sprint

For example, if you described the physical demands of a 100m sprint you would say that it takes anything from 10 to 15 seconds to complete and requires maximum sprinting effort right from the start to the finish line. In other words you work flat-out at a very high intensity for 10 to 15 seconds.

©iStockphoto.com/Greg Ferguson

Energy production for 100m sprint

Based on this evidence you would deduce that nearly all of the energy for this event would be produced anaerobically (without oxygen). This means that anaerobic energy production would be very important for this event and aerobic energy production of very little importance. To prepare a training programme for this event you would therefore concentrate on improving your ability to produce anaerobic energy.

Muscular fitness for 100m sprint

Again, based on the evidence, you would deduce that the most important muscular force for this event would be muscular power and that muscular endurance would be of little importance. This means that in your training programme you would focus on improving your muscular power.

Finally, you would not want your stride length to be restricted and to have freedom around your shoulders for your arm action, so flexibility training would also be an important part of your training programme.

Similarly, if you were asked to plan a physical fitness training programme for a 10km road race, you would need to decide which components of physical fitness are most important for that event. That depends on the physical demands of the event.

Physical demands for 10km road race

A 10km road race will require quick running at the start for perhaps one two minutes, followed by a period of anything from 35 to 45 at a steady pace, then a finish with fast running and a sprint to the line.

Energy production for 10km road race

If you analyse the physical demands of the 10km road race you will deduce that start and finish are high-intensity and you will need to produce energy anaerobically. However, for most of the race you will rely on aerobic energy. This means that the training programme should mostly concentrate on improving your ability to produce aerobic energy with just some work on improving your ability to produce energy anaerobically.

Muscular fitness for 10km road race

Again, based on the evidence you would deduce that the most important muscular force for this event would be muscular endurance and that muscular strength would be of little importance. This means that your training programme should focus on improving muscular endurance.

Flexibility is important for all sports, but relatively speaking it is of little importance for a 10km road race.

 TASK on Components

Purpose

To help you to decide the relative importance of the components of fitness for a range of events, sports or positions within sports.

To help you to analyse the physical fitness demands of events, sports or positions and then based on each analysis rate the importance of the various components of physical fitness for that event, sport or position.

Instructions

Describe the physical demands of the event, sport or position.

Based on this description, rate the relative importance of the components of physical fitness as being either very important, important, of some importance, or of little importance.

Do this for some of the following events, sports, or positions:

- 10,000m
- 1,500m
- high jump
- hockey
- goalkeeper in hockey

- 100m
- marathon
- long jump
- football
- midfield player in football

○ SUMMARY

In this section you have learnt that there are seven different components of physical fitness:

- aerobic energy production
- anaerobic energy production
- muscular power
- muscular strength
- muscular speed
- muscular endurance
- flexibility

You should know and understand the meaning of each component and what determines fitness in that component.

You should also have learnt how to describe the physical demands of a given physical task, event, sport or position within a sport. Based on your description you should be able to rate the relative importance of aerobic and anaerobic energy production for it.

You should also be able to rate the relative importance of muscular power, strength, speed, endurance and flexibility for it.

In doing this you are carrying out the first important step for planning an appropriate and effective exercise or training programme. You decide on the components that are most important for the physical task, event, sport or position, and by concentrating your training on these components you make the training specific or appropriate for the physical task, event, sport or position.

Section 4
Methods

Methods used to develop physical health/wellbeing and peak physical fitness

⭕ Developing aerobic fitness and anaerobic fitness ────

©iStockphoto.com/lisegagne

Running, cycling, swimming, dancing, and rowing are all types of exercise that can be used to develop aerobic or anaerobic energy production. Training methods are simply the different ways that these types of exercise are used. Whether the training method develops aerobic or anaerobic fitness depends on how it is used.

Aerobic and anaerobic training involves working your heart.

Your maximum heart rate (MHR) can be calculated by subtracting your age from 220 if you are male, and from 226 if you are female.

The training methods that you will look at for developing either aerobic or anaerobic fitness are:

- **continuous steady-pace training**
- **fartlek training**
- **interval training**
- **circuit training**

©iStockphoto.com/dsabo

Continuous steady-pace training

This method of training involves **continuous** work at a **steady** rate. Once the heart rate reaches a desired **intensity** (how hard the heart has to work) it is then maintained at that intensity for a period of time, for example 30 minutes.

An example of this kind of training would be running nonstop for 30 minutes at a steady pace, maintaining your heart rate at, for example, 70% MHR.

Continuous steady-pace training is normally associated with developing aerobic fitness.

Fartlek training

©iStockphoto.com/monna

This method involves continuous training but includes working the body at high intensities for varying periods of time. Periods of high-intensity work are followed by periods of recovery. The intensities and the times for which they are maintained are decided during the training, depending on how you feel.

An example of fartlek training would be going for a 30-minute run, during which you break into bursts of fast running for varying lengths of time – anything from ten seconds to two minutes. After a burst of fast running you continue to run slowly, enabling you to recover for the next burst. Fartlek is a Swedish word that means 'speed play'.

Fartlek training can be used to develop aerobic or anaerobic fitness, although it is mostly associated with the former.

Interval training

This method also involves alternating periods of high-intensity work with periods of recovery, but this time the intensity, recovery time and the number of repetitions to be done are decided in advance.

An example of interval training would be running a fixed distance of 200m in a fixed time of 30 seconds, followed by a fixed recovery time of two minutes. This would then be repeated for a fixed number of repetitions, for example five. This would constitute one set (see page 40 for a fuller definition of repetitions and sets).

Interval training can be used to develop aerobic or anaerobic fitness.

Circuit training

This method involves working the body by doing a series of different exercises in a sequence. The intensity or work rate can vary according to the exercises being done.

An example of circuit training would be:

- skipping for 30 seconds followed by 30 seconds rest
- squat thrusts for 30 seconds followed by 30 seconds rest
- shadow-boxing for 30 seconds followed by 30 seconds rest
- sit-ups for 30 seconds followed by 30 seconds rest
- step-ups for 30 seconds followed by 30 seconds rest
- press-ups for 30 seconds followed by 30 seconds rest

The exercises would be done in this sequence and this would be one **circuit**. The circuit could be repeated a number of times.

Circuit training can be used to develop aerobic or anaerobic fitness.

Using the training methods to develop aerobic or anaerobic fitness

Continuous steady-pace, fartlek, interval and circuit training are well-established training methods that have been found to develop either aerobic or anaerobic fitness. People are continually trying different variations of these methods or trying to discover new methods that will work even better.

Simply using a training method is not enough. You must understand how it should be used in order to be effective for developing either aerobic or anaerobic fitness.

The principles for using the training methods are based on **intensity** (how hard you have to work), **time** (how long you have to work) and with some training methods the recovery time you take. They are all **interrelated**.

A **repetition** is a short burst of work/exercise or an exercise like an activity being performed once. After this there will be a rest/recovery period. This may be complete rest where nothing is done, or it may involve doing low-intensity work/exercise.

A **set** is the number of repetitions completed *in a row* before a *significant* rest/recovery period is taken.

Training method	To develop aerobic fitness	To develop anaerobic fitness
Continuous steady-pace training	**Percentage of MHR** (how hard) To be effective the intensity should have the heart working between 55–90% MHR. Whether maintained close to 55 or 90% depends on the individual and the circumstances. **Time** (how long) A workout performed at the appropriate intensity should last at least 20 minutes in order to be effective. **Distance** (how far) A workout performed at the appropriate intensity should cover a distance that would take a minimum of 20 minutes to complete, eg to run 4 miles or to cycle 10km at a steady pace. **Time and distance combined** (how hard, how long, and how far) When you state a distance and the time in which the distance must be completed then you are setting an intensity or work rate. If the distance takes at least 20 minutes to complete and during that time the heart is maintained at a steady rate within the range of 55–90% MHR, then the workout will be effective. **Rest/Recovery** There are not normally rest or recovery times during continuous steady-pace training. Recovery happens at the end of the training. **Repetitions and sets** Repetitions and sets are not normally used in continuous steady-pace training.	Continuous steady-pace training is not normally used to develop anaerobic fitness.

Training method	To develop aerobic fitness	To develop anaerobic fitness
Fartlek training	**Percentage of MHR** (how hard) To be effective the intensity should have the heart working between 55–90% MHR. During bursts of hard work (high intensity) the heart will be worked at 80–90% MHR; during recovery times it will gradually slow down to around 70% MHR.	**Percentage of MHR** (how hard) To be effective bursts of high-intensity work should have the heart working above 90% MHR. This involves working at near maximum effort during these bursts.
	Time (how long) The fartlek workout with its bursts of high-intensity work followed by recovery times should last at least 20 minutes in order to be effective. Overall the intensity of the workout must follow the guidance above.	**Time** (how long) In developing anaerobic fitness the focus shifts from the overall time spent training (eg 30 minutes) to the time spent on each burst of very high-intensity work (eg 30 seconds). Due to the very high intensity of the bursts, they will be relatively short.
	Distance (how far) The fartlek workout should cover a distance that would take a minimum of 20 minutes to complete in order to be effective, eg a 4-mile fartlek run. Overall, the intensity of the workout must also be appropriate.	**Distance** (how far) In developing anaerobic fitness the focus shifts from the overall distance covered to the distance covered during each burst of very high-intensity work. Due to the very high intensity of the bursts, the distance covered during each will be relatively short.
	Time and distance combined (how hard, how long, and how far) When you state a distance and the time in which the distance must be completed then you are setting an intensity or work rate. If the distance takes at least 20 minutes to complete and the heart rate remains within the range of 55–90% MHR throughout the training, then the workout will be effective. During the bursts of hard work the heart rate will rise to 80–90% MHR but will fall during the periods of recovery.	**Time and distance combined** (how hard, how long, and how far) In anaerobic work it is the intensity that is crucial. As you need to work at very high intensities, the distances and times for each burst of very high-intensity work will be relatively short.

Training method	To develop aerobic fitness	To develop anaerobic fitness
Fartlek training	**Rest/Recovery** Fartlek training involves bursts of high-intensity work followed by time to recover. The recovery time normally depends on the intensity of the burst of work. The higher the intensity the longer the recovery period. In developing aerobic fitness the recovery time should normally be no longer than the work time. **Repetitions and sets** Repetitions and sets are not normally used in fartlek training. You will do a number of bursts of high-intensity work, but the number is not normally planned before the training. You do the bursts of work as you feel like doing them so the number can vary. In aerobic compared to anaerobic training you are likely to do more and longer bursts of work but at lower intensities.	**Rest/Recovery** As you do bursts of work at very high intensities you need time to recover from each exertion so that you can complete the next burst of work at the same very high intensity. Recovery times will be longer than work times. The harder and longer the burst of work, the longer the recovery should be. **Repetitions and sets** Repetitions and sets are not normally used in fartlek training. You will do a number of bursts of very high-intensity work, but the number is not normally planned before the training. You do the bursts of work as you feel like doing them so the number can vary. In anaerobic compared to aerobic training you are likely to do fewer and shorter bursts of work but at higher intensities.
Interval training	**Percentage of MHR** (how hard) To be effective each repetition should have the heart working between 80–90% MHR. **Time** (how long) The time to complete one repetition should be anything from 30 seconds to 2 minutes. A workout performed at the appropriate intensity should last at least 20 minutes to be effective.	**Percentage of MHR** (how hard) To be effective each repetition should have the heart working above 90% MHR. This involves working at near maximum or maximum effort for each repetition. **Time** (how long) The time to complete one repetition should be anything from 10 seconds to 1 minute. The intensity of the work is very high so the time working is relatively short.

Training method	To develop aerobic fitness	To develop anaerobic fitness
Interval training	**Distance** (how far) The distance for each repetition will be determined by the type of exercise, eg running or swimming, and the time planned for each repetition. **Time and distance combined** (how hard, how long, and how far) If each repetition has the heart working between 80–90% MHR and the guidance above on time and distance is followed, then the interval training will be effective. **Rest/Recovery** The recovery period after each repetition should be no more than, and preferably less than, the period of high-intensity work. **Repetitions and sets** The total number of repetitions (reps x sets) depends on the intensity of each repetition and the time taken to complete it. For example, in running if you did one repetition of 200m at the same intensity as you did one repetition of 800m, you would expect the total number of repetitions for the workout using 200m to be much higher than the total number of repetitions for the workout using 800m. It could be 200m x 12 repetitions = 2,400m, and 800m x 3 repetitions = 2,400m.	**Distance** (how far) The distance for each repetition will be determined by the type of exercise, eg running or swimming, and the time planned for each repetition. **Time and distance combined** (how hard, how long, and how far) If each repetition has the heart working above 90% MHR and the guidance above on time and distance is followed, then the interval training will be effective. **Rest/Recovery** The recovery period after each repetition should normally be more than the period of very high-intensity work. A ratio of 4:1 is suggested. **Repetitions and sets** The total number of repetitions (reps x sets) depends on the intensity of each repetition and the time taken to complete it. For developing anaerobic fitness the intensity is most important. As you work at very high intensities the time for a repetition is normally below one minute. There is therefore little difference between the total number of repetitions, eg 200m x 3 repetitions = 600m, and 300m x 2 repetitions = 600m. Generally the total number of repetitions is small.

Training method	To develop aerobic fitness	To develop anaerobic fitness
Interval training	Using the same distance of repetition to develop aerobic or anaerobic fitness helps highlight the main differences between an aerobic and anaerobic workout. To develop aerobic fitness there will be a fixed time to complete the distance. This time will be more than the time for anaerobic fitness. The intensity will be moderate to high requiring moderate to hard effort. The recovery between repetitions will be no more than the work time but preferably less. There will be many repetitions done with this intensity	Using the same distance of repetition to develop aerobic or anaerobic fitness helps highlight the main differences between an aerobic and anaerobic workout. To develop anaerobic fitness there will be a fixed time to complete the distance. This time will be less than the time for aerobic fitness. The intensity will be high to very high requiring very hard to maximum effort. The recovery between repetitions will be longer than that used for aerobic fitness, and will be at least four times the length of the work time. Only a small number of repetitions will be done at this intensity.
Circuit training	**Percentage of MHR** (how hard) To be effective the intensity should have the heart working between 55–90% MHR. During bursts of hard work (high intensity) at an exercise station the heart will be worked at 80–90% MHR; during recovery times while moving to the next exercise station it will gradually slow down to around 70% MHR. **Time** (how long) The time at one exercise station should be anything from 30 seconds to 2 minutes. The overall circuit with its periods of work at each exercise station followed by recovery times should last at least 20 minutes in order to be effective. Overall, the intensity of the workout must follow the guidance above.	**Percentage of MHR** (how hard) To be effective work at each exercise station should have the heart working above 90% MHR. This involves working at near maximum or maximum effort at each exercise station. **Time** (how long) The time at one exercise station should be anything from 10 seconds to 1 minute. The intensity of the work will be very high so the time at each exercise station will be relatively short.

Training method	To develop aerobic fitness	To develop anaerobic fitness
Circuit training	**Distance** (how far) Distance is not normally associated with circuit training. **Time and distance combined** (how hard, how long, and how far) Time and distance combined are not normally associated with circuit training. **Rest/Recovery** The recovery period after each exercise station should be no more than, and preferably less than, the period of work at the exercise station. **Repetitions and sets** The total number of repetitions done at an exercise station depends on the intensity of the exercise and the time to be spent at each exercise station. It is best to have exercises of moderate intensity and to decide a time for each exercise station rather than decide a number of repetitions. This time is likely to be between 30 seconds and 1 minute. A set would be the equivalent of one circuit.	**Distance** (how far) Distance is not normally associated with circuit training. **Time and distance combined** (how hard, how long, and how far) Time and distance combined are not normally associated with circuit training. **Rest/Recovery** The recovery period after each exercise station should normally be more than the period of very high-intensity work. A ratio of 4:1 is suggested. **Repetitions and sets** The total number of repetitions done at an exercise station depends on the intensity of the exercise and the time to be spent at each exercise station. It is best to have exercises of high intensity and to decide a time for each exercise station rather than decide a number of repetitions. This time is likely to be 10 to 20 seconds. A set would be the equivalent of one circuit.

Developing muscular power, muscular strength, muscular speed and muscular endurance

Any exercise that works our skeletal muscles can be used to develop either muscular power, strength, speed or endurance. Training methods are simply different ways by which these can be developed. Whether the training method develops muscular power, strength, speed or endurance depends on how it is used.

©iStockphoto.com/Mike_Kiev

The training methods you will study in this section are:

- **isotonic weight-training**
- **circuit training**
- **assault-course-type training**
- **isometric training**

Isotonic weight-training

©iStockphoto.com/Dr Grounds

Isotonic weight-training involves a muscle or group of muscles working against a resistance (a weight) and movement of body parts takes place. Weight-training exercises usually involve the muscle working **concentrically** where the muscle gets shorter and more bulky as it works, and then **eccentrically** where the muscle gets longer and less bulky as it works.

An example of an isotonic weight-training exercise would be a **biceps curl**. In this exercise you hold, with your palms facing forward, a barbell with an appropriate weight. The barbell rests by your thighs and your arms are straight. You lift the weight by bending your arms at the elbow. The weight is raised up until the barbell touches your chest. It is then lowered by straightening your arms until the barbell once again rests by your thighs.

Isotonic weight-training can be done by using **free weights**, by using **fixed weights**, or by using machines that provide a resistance.

With free weights you attach weights to a barbell or dumbbell or you can have pre-manufactured dumbbell weights. These weights can be moved freely about the area. With fixed weights the weights are part of a machine and they are moved by lever or pulley systems. Some machines provide resistances without the need for actual weights.

Isotonic weight-training can be used to develop muscular power, strength, speed or endurance. This training method is the most easily adapted to specifically develop these components of muscular fitness.

Circuit training

Circuit training involves working the body by doing a series of different exercises in a sequence. For more information, see Section 4, page 40.

You have already explored how circuit training can be used to develop aerobic or anaerobic fitness. This training method can also be used to develop muscular power, strength, speed or endurance, and is most associated with developing general muscular fitness.

Assault-course-type training

This kind of training involves working the muscles by getting you to get over objects, get under objects, carry objects, climb, swing, jump, and run.

The army uses this kind of training with their new recruits.

This training method can be used to develop muscular power, strength, speed or endurance, and is most associated with developing general muscular fitness.

Isometric training

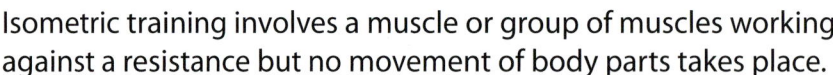

Isometric training involves a muscle or group of muscles working against a resistance but no movement of body parts takes place.

An example of this kind of exercise would be putting your back against a wall and putting yourself into a seated position which you would then hold.

Your muscles are working to hold you in this position, but no movement of body parts takes place.

This training method is limited to developing muscular strength or endurance in the position held.

Using the training methods to develop muscular power, strength, speed or endurance

Isotonic weight-training, circuit training, assault-course-type training and isometric training are well-established training methods that have been found to work (although isometric is limited). People are continually trying different variations of the methods or trying to discover new methods that will work even better.

As with developing aerobic and anaerobic fitness, simply using a training method is not enough. You must understand how it should be used in order to be effective for developing muscular power, strength, speed or endurance.

The principles for using the training methods are based on intensity (how hard you have to work), the time you have to work or the number of repetitions and sets that you have to do (how long you have to work), and the recovery time you take (recovery/rest). They are all interrelated.

Intensity

In developing muscular fitness your muscles need to work against a resistance. The resistance will be different according to what type of muscular fitness you wish to develop.

The resistance can be a weight expressed in kilograms (kg). For one exercise you could lift 20kg, and for another you could lift 10kg. If you wanted to develop another component of muscular fitness, the weights you lift would change.

The weight (or resistance) can also be expressed as a **Repetition Maximum (RM)**. This is the maximum weight you can lift a certain number of times. For example, 1RM is the maximum weight that can be lifted only once or for one repetition, and 10RM is the maximum weight that can be lifted for 10 repetitions but no more.

The advantage of using the RM method for expressing the weight is that it allows the principles for developing the components of muscular fitness to be explained and applied to a group of people without referring to specific weights. Everyone can be told that the weight they are to lift is 15RM – the maximum weight they can lift for 15 repetitions but no more. Everyone must discover what that weight is for them. In practice that could be 5kg for one person, 10kg for another person, and 20kg for another. They all lift different weights but for each of them that is the weight that is appropriate for them (15RM).

In some training methods your body weight is used to provide the resistance instead. In these cases words can be used to describe the resistance or the intensity of the exercise. For example, a high-intensity exercise would be hard and require considerable effort to move your body weight (eg doing a press-up with your feet on a table and your hands on the floor) whereas a moderate intensity exercise would be easier and require less effort to move your body weight (eg doing a press-up with your feet on the floor and your hands on a wall).

Repetitions, sets, time and recovery time

A repetition is an exercise performed once. A set is the number of continuous repetitions completed before a significant rest is taken. Instead of doing a fixed number of repetitions you may do as many repetitions as possible in a fixed time, for example 20 seconds. Recovery/rest time is the amount of rest taken between sets.

Using isotonic weight-training to develop muscular fitness

Fitness	RM	Weight (% of 1RM)	Reps	Sets	Rest	Frequency per week
Muscular power	1–5	85–100	1–5	4–8	3–5 mins	3–5 days
Muscular strength	6–12	70–84	6–12	3–4	1–3 mins	3–5 days
Muscular endurance	13–25	50–69	13–25	1–3	30–60 secs	3–5 days
Muscular speed	30–60	20–40	15–25	1–2	3–5 mins	3–5 days

Using circuit training to develop muscular fitness

Fitness	Exercise intensity	Reps	Sets	Rest	Frequency per week
Muscular power	Very high-intensity or very hard exercises	1–5	4–8	3–5 mins	3–5 days
Muscular strength	High-intensity or hard exercises	6–12	3–4	1–3 mins	3–5 days
Muscular endurance	Moderate intensity or somewhat hard exercises	13–25	1–3	30–60 secs	3–5 days
Muscular speed	Limited intensity or easy exercise, performed fast	15–25	1–2	3–5 mins	3–5 days

Using assault-course-type training to develop muscular fitness

The challenges in assault course-type training can be designed to work different parts of the body and develop muscular power, strength or endurance depending on the amount of effort/force required by the person. For example, having to use full force to run and jump from a height to clear a ditch, then absorb the landing would develop muscular power in the legs. Carrying another person or carrying a heavy load across a ditch would develop muscular strength in the legs. Running from one challenge to the next to complete the course would develop muscular endurance in the legs. The demands of the challenges and the length of time a person works on them determines the focus of the training.

©iStockphoto.com/ssuni

The same general principles that apply to isotonic weight-training also apply to assault course-type training. The harder the challenges the more likely the training will develop muscular strength and power and the time spent doing the course will not be as long. The easier the challenges the more likely the training will develop muscular endurance and the time spent doing the course will be longer.

Using isometric training to develop muscular fitness

With isometric training the muscle or group of muscles work but there is no movement of body parts. This means that the muscular strength or muscular endurance is only developed in the muscle in the position in which it is held. This limits the use made of isometric training as most sports are dynamic and involve movement, but it can be used in some sports such as gymnastics where static positions need to be held.

©iStockphoto.com/barsik

The same general principles that apply to the other methods also apply to isometric training. The greater the resistance the more likely it will develop strength, while less intense resistances which are held longer will develop muscular endurance.

Developing flexibility

Any physical activity or exercise that stretches our skeletal muscles can be used to develop flexibility. Training methods are simply different ways by which flexibility can be developed.

The training methods that you will look at for developing flexibility are **static flexibility training**, performed actively or passively, and **active/ballistic** or **dynamic flexibility training**.

Static flexibility training performed actively or passively

This method involves slowly stretching the muscle to its limit and then holding it in this stretched position for a time.

An example would be sitting on the floor with your legs straight, then slowly reaching forwards towards your toes until you feel mild tension in your muscles. You would then hold this position for a number of seconds.

If you hold on to your lower legs and pull your body down to keep the muscles stretched and under mild tension then you are performing the static flexibility exercise actively. If you get another person to push down on your shoulders to keep the muscles stretched and under mild tension then you are performing the exercise passively. Performed actively, you provide the force to stretch the muscle and hold it in that position. Performed passively, another person provides this force.

To develop flexibility effectively, static flexibility exercises should be held under mild tension for 20 to 30 seconds. Two or three repetitions of the exercise may be done. The muscles should be relaxed during the rest/recovery period between the repetitions.

Active/ballistic or dynamic flexibility training

This method involves bouncing, jerking or swinging body parts in order to put the muscle in a stretched position and produce greater muscle length.

An example would be bending forwards to touch your toes, then bouncing up and down to stretch the muscles.

In ballistic flexibility exercises, the force to stretch the muscle is provided by the bouncing, jerking or swinging movement. It is possible to damage a muscle using this method, so it is not recommended for health-related flexibility.

To develop your flexibility, the exercise can be done for 20 to 60 seconds or for 20 to 60 repetitions.

This method can be used by sportspeople whose movements involve this type of flexibility, for example high jumpers.

TASK on Methods

Purpose

To develop your ability to apply principles appropriately to make various training methods effective.

To develop your ability to evaluate whether principles have been applied appropriately.

Instructions

Provide the information that demonstrates you understand what the following training methods involve and what principles should be applied to make them effective for the given purpose.

- fartlek training to develop aerobic fitness
- interval training to develop anaerobic fitness
- isotonic weight-training to develop muscular power
- circuit training to develop muscular endurance
- active static flexibility training to develop flexibility

Look at other people's answers. Judge their understanding of the various types of training and how well they have applied the principles appropriately for the given purpose.

SUMMARY

©iStockphoto.com/monna

You should now know and understand:

- that physical fitness involves the following components – aerobic fitness, anaerobic fitness, muscular power, muscular strength, muscular endurance, muscular speed and flexibility

- that there is a variety of training methods which can be used to develop or improve your physical fitness in these components

- how these training methods should be used in order to be effective in developing specific components

Section 5
Principles

Principles used to develop physical health/wellbeing and peak physical fitness

In this section you will learn the principles you need to follow when using your selected and appropriate training methods in order to develop your physical fitness gradually towards your peak. These are known as the **principles of training** and must be applied to training programmes for them to be effective. They are:

- **specificity**
- **overload**
- **progressive overload**
- **rest/recovery**
- **variety**
- **peaking**
- **maintenance and reversibility**

◯ Specificity

The effects of training are very specific. If you want to improve your physical fitness for a particular event, sport or position within a sport, then your training and training methods must match, as much as possible, the physical fitness demands of that event, sport or position.

At its simplest this means that if you want to train for a 10km road run then your training should be, for the most part, running. If you want to train to improve your swimming performances then your training must focus on swimming.

You need to be able to analyse the relative importance of the components of physical fitness for an event, sport or position, then explain what the emphasis in the training programme would be.

For example, if you had to devise a training programme to run a marathon you would look at the physical demands of the event. The marathon requires a person to run aerobically for anything from 2½ to 3½ hours and during that time the legs are continually working, pounding the ground. This means the emphasis in the training programme would be on developing aerobic fitness and muscular endurance through running.

If you had to devise a training programme to run 100m you would once again look at the demands of the event. The 100m requires flat-out or maximum effort for anything from 10 to 15 seconds. It also requires strength and power in running. This means the emphasis in the training programme would be on developing strength, power and anaerobic fitness.

Imagine having to devise the training programme for a decathlete in track and field athletics. You would have to consider the physical fitness demands for the following 10 events and make sure the decathlete is prepared to perform well in all of them: 100m, long jump, shot put, high jump, 400m, 110m hurdles, discus, pole vault, javelin and 1,500m.

When you consider health, the most important components of physical fitness are aerobic fitness, muscular endurance and flexibility. If you want to have an exercise programme that develops and maintains physical health/wellbeing then it must include exercise for these three areas – this is applying the principle of specificity to health.

Overload

If you want to develop your physical fitness in any of the components, then you must work the body systems harder than they are being worked at present. In other words you must **overload**.

©iStockphoto.com/petech

For example, if you were doing continuous steady-pace running for three nights per week at an intensity of 70% MHR and for 20 minutes each run then you would have achieved a certain level of aerobic fitness. If you wanted to improve on this level then you would have to apply the principle of overload. You could do this by running an extra night per week, or running at an intensity of 80% MHR instead of 70% on one or more of the runs, or running for 25 minutes instead of 20 minutes for one or more of the runs. If you did any one of these or any combination of these you would have applied the principle of overload.

The overload puts added stress on the body, and the body gradually adapts to cope with it. This adaptation is due to the body systems changing and becoming more efficient. Because of this increased efficiency (improved physical fitness) what was originally a stress on the body is no longer a stress but normal.

The skill in applying the principle of overload is to add enough stress to make a difference and make the body adapt, but not to add too much stress which could lead to fatigue or injury.

There must be a minimum overload on the body to gain a health benefit – in other words, a minimum frequency of exercise per week, a minimum intensity of exercise, and a minimum time that should be spent exercising. This minimum overload is known as the **FITT principle**:

- F – minimum Frequency
- I – minimum Intensity
- T – minimum Time
- T – Type of exercise

The type of exercise ties in with the principle of specificity.

The following table shows the minimum overload for a health benefit to be gained in the three health-related components of physical fitness.

Activity for health	The FITT principle (minimum overload to gain a health benefit)			
	F = Frequency	I = Intensity	T = Time	T = Type of exercise
Aerobic exercise	3 sessions/week	55% or 70% MHR	20 minutes	Continuous
Muscular endurance exercise	3 sessions/week	Moderate to hard exercises with many repetitions	Cover major muscles	Weights, circuit training or exercises
Flexibility exercise	3 sessions/week	Mild tension felt in stretched muscles	Cover muscles surrounding major joints	Static flexibility exercises

The lower intensity suggested for aerobic exercise (55% MHR) would be used with individuals who are frail and have not exercised for a long time. For most young people 70% MHR is a more appropriate threshold.

The table above refers to physical health/wellbeing, and shows the minimum amount of exercise that should be done for a health benefit to be gained. However, it is much better for your physical health/wellbeing if you are involved in an hour of moderate aerobic activity every day and do more than three muscular endurance and flexibility sessions per week.

The minimum amount of exercise that needs to be done for an improvement to be made in any of the components of physical fitness is referred to as the **threshold of training**. If you cross this with your overload then your fitness will improve.

Progressive overload

If any of your body systems are subjected to an overload through training then they adapt to cope more efficiently with the overload. In other words you become fitter. If you want to become even fitter you overload again, and as before your body systems adapt to cope. This principle of overloading and the body adapting, then overloading again and the body adapting, is the principle of **progressive overload**.

It is important that the overload at the beginning of the training programme is at an appropriate level for the individual and their circumstances, and that the overload is increased gradually and sensibly over the training programme.

This can be achieved by:

- increasing the frequency of the training, for example training more days in the week
- increasing the intensity of the training, for example working harder during a training session
- increasing the length of time you train for in a session, for example training for 40 minutes instead of 30 minutes

You can use one or any combination of these to increase the overload.

To apply the principle of progressive overload effectively you need to understand the components of physical fitness and how the training methods are used to develop these components.

For example, the way you progressively overload to improve muscular strength differs somewhat from the way you progressively overload to improve muscular endurance.

For **muscular strength** you would first look at increasing the resistance or the weight to be lifted – the number of repetitions would stay much the same.

For **muscular endurance** you would first look at increasing the time you spend on each exercise or increasing the number of repetitions – the resistance or weight would stay much the same.

Rest/Recovery

You will benefit from a hard workout only if you allow your muscles time to recover and your body time to replace fuel used up.

A recovery period or a rest day does not necessarily mean that you do nothing. You may still train but at a low intensity. This training at a relaxed and easy pace may even help recovery.

The best guidance for the balance between work in training and rest/recovery is the harder you work in training then the more time you should allow for rest and recovery.

Variety

You are less likely to become psychologically and physically bored and less likely to stay on a plateau without improving if a variety of training methods and venues are used.

If you are exercising to maintain aerobic fitness for physical health/wellbeing then it doesn't really matter if you get this variety by going swimming one day, going cycling another day and going running another day. However, if you are training for a particular event or sport, for example a 10km road run, then the cycling and swimming may not be particularly helpful to you as your preparation. In this case the variety should be provided by changing the training methods and/or the venues.

For example, you could do a continuous steady-pace run in the park for one session, a fartlek run in the forest for another, and an interval training session on the 400m track for another.

You have variety through the range of training methods and venues yet the principle of specificity has still been applied.

Peaking

When you start a training programme you often have a **foundation phase**; this would be followed by a **development phase**; then you would have a **sharpening phase**; and finally you have a **peaking phase**.

The aim of training is to prepare your body so that it is at its peak level of physical fitness to allow you to perform at your very best on the day of an important competition. The principle of peaking covers the final stages prior to the competition.

The idea is that in the period prior to an important competition you perform much less work, but what work you do is at a high intensity. Then, some days before the competition you ease right off or taper off with your training to allow your muscles complete recovery and your fuel stores to be full.

Maintenance/Reversibility

If you want to maintain your level of physical fitness then you need to continue to train.

If you stop training then the biological adaptations produced by the body will be reversed and you will lose your level of physical fitness.

 **TASK on Principles**

Purpose

To help you analyse information and make decisions based on your analysis.

To help you to apply principles appropriately and effectively.

Instructions

Analyse the physical demands for the following events, sports or positions within a sport then demonstrate how the principle of specificity should be applied to a training programme for each.

- 10,000m track race
- long jump
- tennis
- a midfield player in a team game

Copy out the tables below and over the page. Using this information as your baseline or starting point, demonstrate how the principles of overload and progressive overload should be applied to make each training programme effective. Explain your decisions in each case.

Week	Type/method	Intensity	Time	Frequency
Baseline	Steady-pace running for aerobic fitness	70% MHR	15 mins	2 days/week
Weeks 1–3	Steady-pace running for aerobic fitness			
Weeks 4–6	Steady-pace running for aerobic fitness			

Week	Type/method	Intensity	Time	Frequency
Baseline	Interval training for anaerobic fitness	200m in 30 secs. Recovery time 1 min between each.	5 repetitions	3 days/week
Weeks 1–3	Interval training for anaerobic fitness			
Weeks 4–6	Interval training for anaerobic fitness			

Week	Type/method	Intensity	Time	Frequency
Baseline	Weight-training exercise to improve power	20kg	5 repetitions 3 sets	3 days/week
Weeks 1–3	Weight-training exercise to improve power			
Weeks 4–6	Weight-training exercise to improve power			

Week	Type/method	Intensity	Time	Frequency
Baseline	Weight-training exercise to improve endurance	10kg	15 repetitions 1 set	2 days/week
Weeks 1–3	Weight-training exercise to improve endurance			
Weeks 4–6	Weight-training exercise to improve endurance			

◯ SUMMARY

In Section 4 you learnt a range of training methods that can be used to develop the components of physical fitness.

In this section you have learnt the principles of training that must be applied to these training methods to create an effective training programme.

Section 6
Monitoring & assessment

©iStockphoto.com/lovleah

How monitoring and assessment are used when developing physical health/ wellbeing and peak physical fitness

◯ Purpose of monitoring and assessment

The assessment and monitoring of your level of physical fitness in the relevant components for health or your event, sport or position in your sport is worthwhile doing before, during and at the end of your training programme.

Monitoring and assessment helps you to:

- judge your level of fitness before you begin your training programme
- discover strengths and weaknesses
- set realistic short-term and intermediate goals/targets
- stay motivated
- judge the progress being made during the training programme
- adjust your training programme in light of the information gained from the assessments

There are many different ways to monitor and assess the effectiveness of your training programme. Whatever means is used you must be clear on how progress or success will be measured.

◯ 'Listening' to your body

You can 'listen' to your body to judge whether your aerobic exercise/ training is effective. You know your exercise/training is working if:

- you feel that you are no longer out of breath when you would have been before
- you have more energy than you would have had before
- you are able to lift, push or pull things much more easily than before
- you are able to bend, twist, turn or stretch much more easily than before

Resting pulse rate

You can use your **resting pulse rate** to judge whether your aerobic exercise/training is effective. Your pulse rate is the number of times that your heart beats in one minute.

To use this test you need to take your resting pulse rate before you start your exercise/training programme. It is best taken first thing in the morning when you wake up. Once you are into your programme you can take your resting pulse rate as before.

If it is lower than before you started your programme then you know that the programme is effective.

Recovery rate

You can use your **recovery rate** to judge whether your aerobic exercise/training is effective. Your recovery rate is the time it takes for your heart rate to return to a set rate (eg 80bpm) after having completed a set piece of work.

To use this test you need to do a set test or piece of work, then record your recovery rate. Once you are into your programme you do the same test or piece of work and record your recovery rate once again.

If the rate is quicker now than it was before you started your programme then you know that the programme is effective.

Distance and time

You can use distance and time to judge whether your aerobic exercise/training is effective. You can either set the distance and measure the time it takes to complete that distance, or you can set the time and measure the distance completed in that time.

As with the other assessments you must do the test before you start the programme and then use the same test again during it.

If you set the distance and measured the time then the programme is effective if you can now run the distance in a faster time.

If you set the time and measured the distance then the programme is regarded as effective if you are now able to run further in the set time.

Repetitions completed

To assess your level of local muscular fitness (eg the stomach muscles or the arm muscles) it is possible to measure the total number of repetitions of an exercise that can be done before fatigue sets in, or you can measure the number of repetitions that can be done in a fixed time. To use this test you need to count the number of repetitions that you can complete for a fixed exercise in a fixed time before you start your exercise/training programme, and then again once you are into the programme. If the programme is effective you would expect to now be able to do more repetitions in the fixed time.

Measuring range of movement

To assess your level of flexibility at joints you can measure the range of movement that you have. For example, the sit and reach test measures the range of movement you have in bending forwards. To use such a test you need to measure your range of movement before you start your exercise/training programme. Once you are into your programme you use the same test again. If the programme is effective then you would now expect to have a greater range of movement.

Principles behind fair assessments

If your testing is to be valid and reliable and allow you to compare results then there are certain principles that must be followed.

You should know and understand the following:

- The tests selected (or designed by you) should be suitable for the purpose. If you want to assess aerobic fitness then the test must be able to do that. If you want to assess flexibility then the test must be able to do that.

- The protocol (procedures and rules) for the tests must be followed strictly. It would not be fair to compare results if the test was done differently on separate occasions.

- The same tests should be used before, during and after the training programme. If you want to measure your progress or to judge the effectiveness of your training programme then the same tests must be used on all occasions to allow a fair comparison of results to be made.

- The tests should be carried out under the same, or similar conditions, each time they are used. It would not be fair to compare the results of a 10 x 5m sprint test if one time the test was performed inside on a non-slip floor and the next time performed outside on wet slippy grass.

Tests used to assess levels of physical fitness

There are hundreds of tests for assessing the components of fitness. They range from expensive and elaborate tests done in a laboratory to simple field tests that can be done at home. There are advantages and disadvantages for all tests.

You have to be able to design or select appropriate tests and apply the principles on the previous page to be able to assess progress in any of the components of physical fitness.

Whether you design a test of your own or select a recognised test appropriate for a given situation or component of physical fitness, you must be able to show that you can apply the principles on the previous page so that progress can be monitored.

You should be able to:

- analyse the situation and decide which component(s) of fitness should be tested

- design or select a test that would be appropriate for the situation and the component of fitness. You should be able to explain why the test is appropriate.

- describe what equipment is needed to administer the test

- describe the protocol for the test (the instructions to be given on how to do the test and the rules for the test)

- explain how the test is measured and recorded

- explain how progress can be measured through using the test regularly during your training programme

TASK 1 on Monitoring & assessment

Purpose

To help you research information on tests that are suitable for the assessment of the components of physical fitness.

Instructions

Use books, fitness magazines and the internet to find tests that are suitable for assessing the components of physical fitness – aerobic, anaerobic, power, strength, speed, endurance and flexibility.

Select at least one test for each component and note:

- the equipment needed to administer the test

- the protocol for the test

- how the test is measured and recorded

- how progress can be measured through using the test regularly during a training programme

▷ TASK 2 on Monitoring & assessment

Purpose

To help you apply the principles of assessment to allow progress to be monitored.

Instructions

For each of (a) – (f) below:

- ● analyse the situation and decide which component(s) of fitness should be tested.
- ● design or select a test that would be appropriate for the situation and the component of fitness. Explain why the test is appropriate.
- ● describe what equipment is needed to administer the test.
- ● describe the protocol for the test.
- ● explain how the test is measured and recorded.
- ● explain how progress can be measured through using the test regularly during the training programme.

(a) An athlete wants to start training to perform well in a 5,000m road race.

(b) A group of midfield games players want to start training to improve their ability to work anaerobically.

(c) A netball player wants to start training to improve the strength of her arms to help her with her passing.

(d) A group of volleyball players want to start training to improve their ability to jump high at the net.

(e) A group of teenagers want to improve the 'tone' of their abdominals or stomach muscles.

(f) A diver wants to improve his piked position for his dives.

◯ SUMMARY

In previous sections you have learnt the components of physical fitness, the training methods used to develop these components, and the principles of training that must be applied for training programmes to be effective.

In this section you have learnt how you can monitor progress in the development of the components.

©iStockphoto.com/Grafissimo

Section 7
Effects

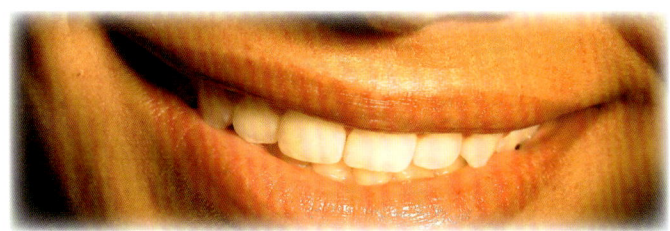

How the methods and principles used to develop physical health/wellbeing and peak physical fitness affect selected body systems

In this section you will learn the immediate effects that exercise has on the **respiratory**, **circulatory**, **musculatory**, **skeletal** and **digestive** systems.

You will also learn the physical changes that occur in the respiratory, circulatory, musculatory and skeletal systems as a result of effective training over a period of time. It is these physical or biological changes that allow your body to work more efficiently (they make you fitter) and thus enable you to perform better.

To understand the physical changes you should know the basic anatomy, physiology and roles of the body systems.

◯ Respiratory system

The respiratory system transfers oxygen to the blood, and carbon dioxide and water vapour from the blood to the atmosphere.

Main parts

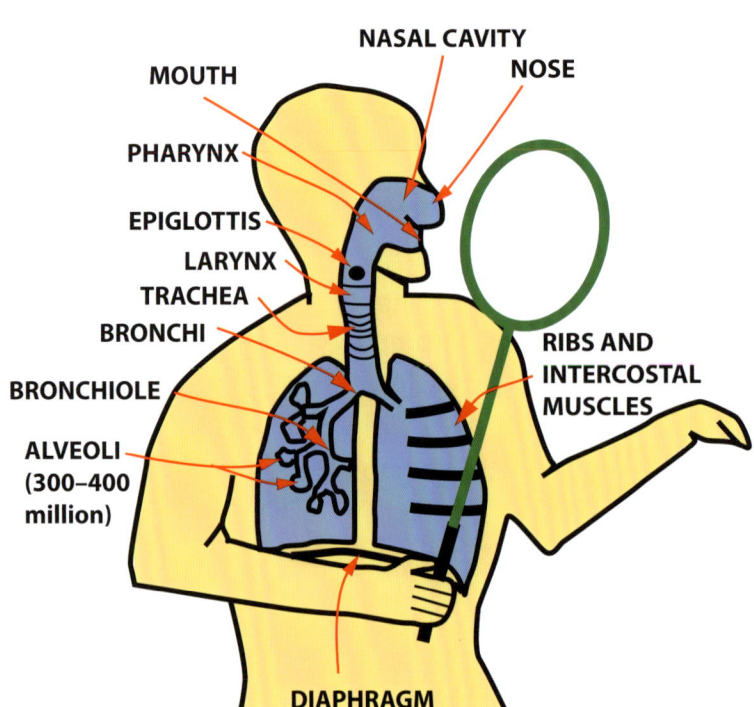

The **trachea**, **bronchi** and **bronchioles** are lined with a **mucous membrane** and **cilia**. The mucous traps dust and dirt and the cilia push this mucous up to the back of the throat where it is swallowed or coughed up.

The **alveoli** are the air sacs where the gaseous exchange of oxygen and carbon dioxide takes place.

How oxygen gets from the outside air into the blood

Inspiration

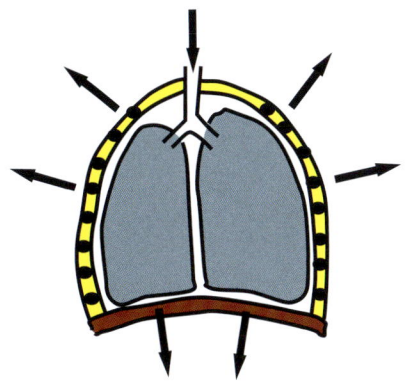

The **intercostal** muscles contract, pulling the ribs up and out. The **diaphragm** contracts pulling itself down. The volume of the **chest cavity** increases and air pressure drops, so air (oxygen) rushes into the alveoli of the lungs to equalise the pressure.

Diffusion

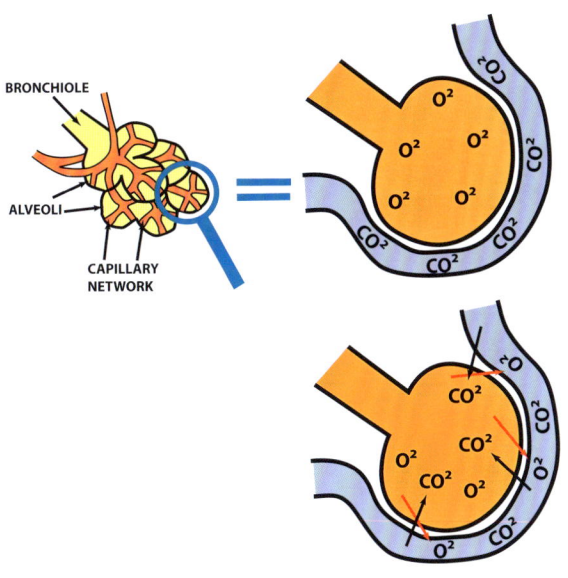

BRONCHIOLE

ALVEOLI

CAPILLARY NETWORK

After breathing in, the alveoli have a high concentration of oxygen, while blood **capillaries** have a low concentration. Oxygen diffuses from the alveoli into the blood capillaries to even out the concentration, while carbon dioxide diffuses from the capillaries into the alveoli. The natural movement of molecules to spread evenly through a liquid is called the process of **diffusion**.

Control of respiration

The **respiratory centre** in the brain detects the amount of carbon dioxide in the blood. The **autonomic nervous system** then adjusts the rate and depth of breathing according to the level of carbon dioxide detected.

Factors influencing performance

Vital capacity

Vital capacity is the maximum amount of air we can breathe out in one breath having breathed in as deeply as we can. It is usually 4 to 5 litres for men and 3 to 4 litres for women. Endurance athletes can have vital capacities of 6 to 7 litres.

Ventilation

Ventilation is the amount of air breathed in and out during a minute.

Ventilation = Frequency of breaths/minute x Volume of air taken in in each breath

These factors are controlled by your genetic potential, the development of your vital capacity, and your respiratory muscles.

Short-term or immediate effects of training on the respiratory system

With exercise, you breathe faster and deeper. In other words your ventilation increases to meet the demands of the exercise.

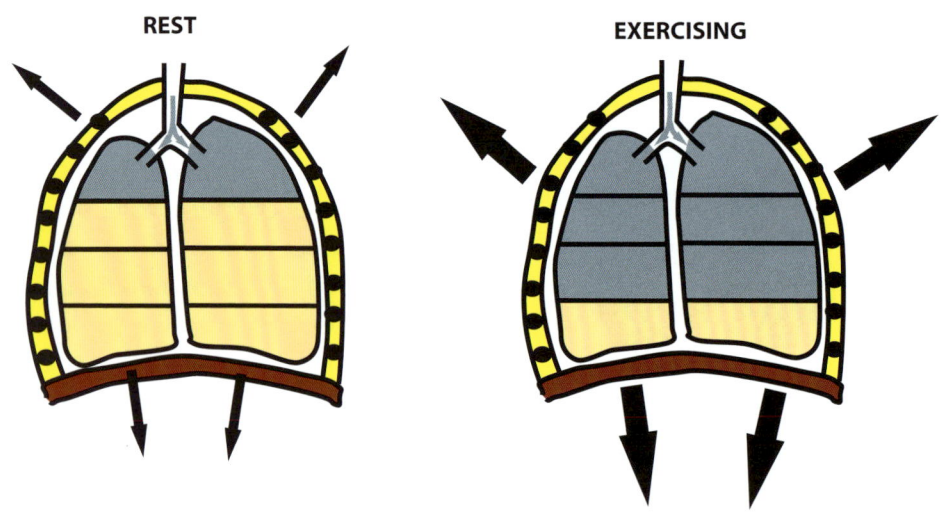

REST   EXERCISING

At rest:

Ventilation =12 breaths/min x 2 litres of air each breath

V = 24 litres/minute

Exercising:

Ventilation = 20 breaths/min x 6 litres of air each breath

V =120 litres/minute

It is more efficient to increase our ventilation through deeper breaths than through breathing faster.

Long-term effects of training on the respiratory system

As a result of regular aerobic endurance training, the intercostal muscles and diaphragm become stronger. This means your vital capacity and ventilation improve. You can get more oxygen in and out of the lungs with each breath and over a period of time, so you can work harder and keep working for longer without tiring.

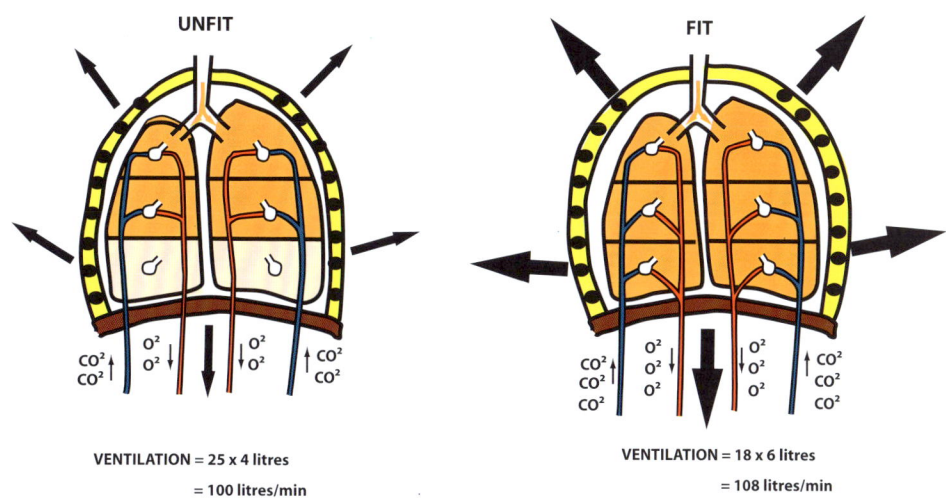

As a result of regular aerobic endurance training the surface area for gaseous exchange is increased. This means your diffusion capacity increases. Alveoli in the lungs which had a poor blood supply get an increased capillary network.

This means that for aerobic tasks it is now easier for you to work at a given work rate than before, and you can work longer and harder than before.

Circulatory system

The circulatory system transports things in the blood, to all parts of the body. The blood carries:

- **red blood cells** (oxygen)
- **white blood cells** (fight infection)
- **platelets** (blood clotting)
- **nutrients** (fuel for energy)
- **carbon dioxide** (waste)
- **urea** (waste)
- **hormones** (regulate body)
- **fibrinogen** (blood clotting)
- **excess heat** (waste)

How the blood flows around the body

The heart pumps the blood round the body. The blood is carried in blood vessels called **arteries**, **veins** and **capillaries**. Capillaries are the smallest blood vessels with walls only one cell thick. This allows for the process of diffusion to take place between the blood and the muscle cells. Oxygen and nutrients diffuse from the blood into the muscle cells and urea like carbon dioxide or **lactic acid** diffuses from the muscle cells into the blood.

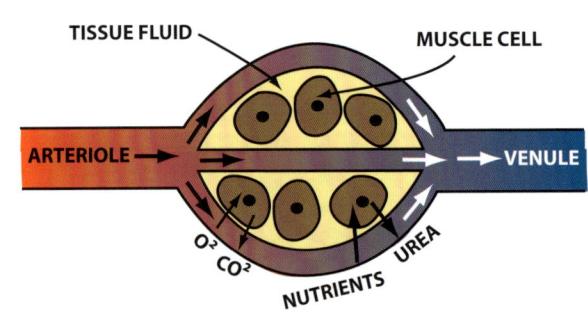

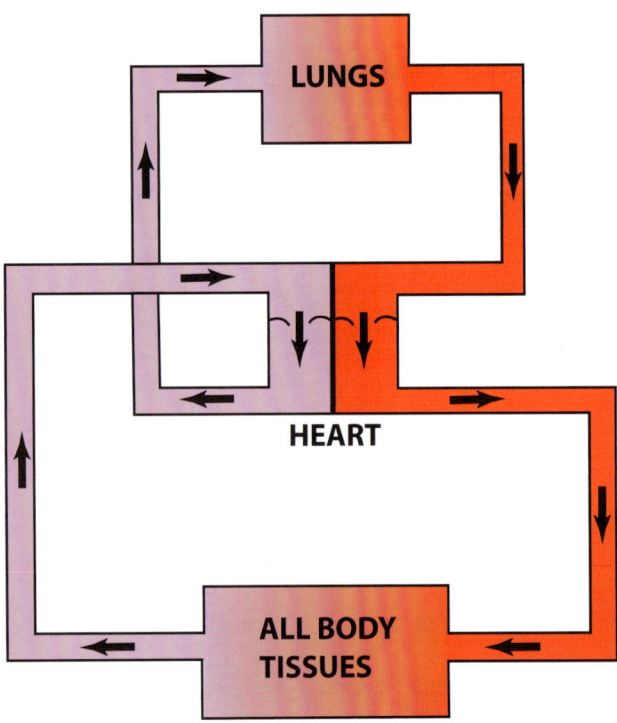

The blood travels from the heart in two circuits. In the **pulmonary circuit** the blood travels from the right side of the heart to the lungs, then back to the left side of the heart. In the **systemic circuit** the blood travels from the left side of the heart to all parts of the body, then back to the right side of the heart. And so it goes on – to the lungs and back, to the body and back – round and round in two 'closed circuits'.

Factors influencing performance

Stroke volume is the amount of blood pumped out from the left **ventricle** per beat.

Cardiac output is the amount of blood pumped out from the left side of the heart in one minute.

These factors are controlled by your genetic potential and the development of your heart and circulatory system.

Control of circulation

The **sinoatrial node** (the heart pacemaker) controls cardiac output. The autonomic nervous system adjusts this according to the demands made by the working muscles.

Short-term or immediate effects of exercise on the circulatory system

Cardiac output increases. The stroke volume and the heart rate increase to meet the demands.

Blood flow is largely diverted to the muscles. The muscles receive 80–85% compared to 15–20% during rest.

During exercise organs such as the stomach, intestines and kidneys with less urgent needs receive only a small amount.

The working muscles take more oxygen from the blood. The muscles take 17ml/100ml compared to 6ml/100ml when resting.

Blood acidity increases because of the amount of lactic acid circulating in the blood.

The blood plasma volume usually decreases because of increased sweating.

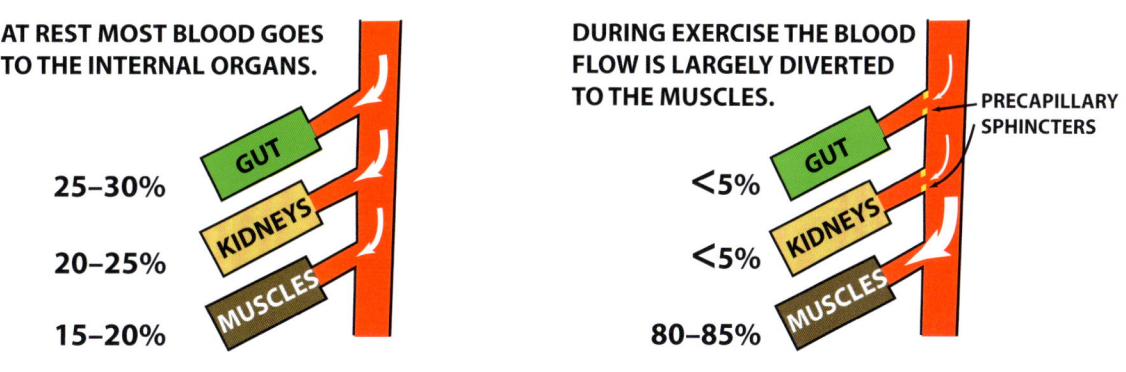

AT REST MOST BLOOD GOES TO THE INTERNAL ORGANS.

GUT 25–30%
KIDNEYS 20–25%
MUSCLES 15–20%

DURING EXERCISE THE BLOOD FLOW IS LARGELY DIVERTED TO THE MUSCLES.

PRECAPILLARY SPHINCTERS

GUT <5%
KIDNEYS <5%
MUSCLES 80–85%

DURING EXERCISE CORONARY BLOOD FLOW INCREASES x 5.
BLOOD FLOW TO THE BRAIN REMAINS CONSTANT (REST OR EXERCISING).

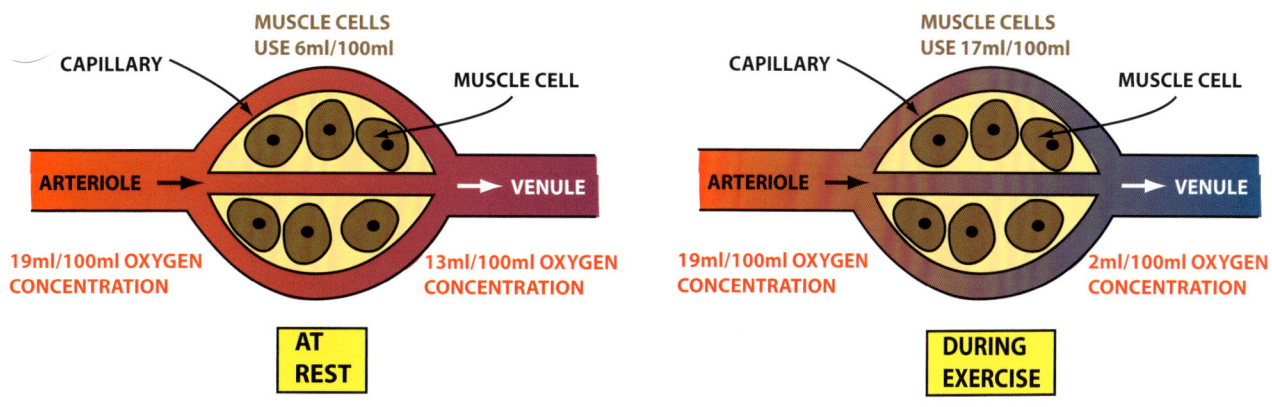

MUSCLE CELLS USE 6ml/100ml
CAPILLARY
MUSCLE CELL
ARTERIOLE
VENULE
19ml/100ml OXYGEN CONCENTRATION
13ml/100ml OXYGEN CONCENTRATION
AT REST

MUSCLE CELLS USE 17ml/100ml
CAPILLARY
MUSCLE CELL
ARTERIOLE
VENULE
19ml/100ml OXYGEN CONCENTRATION
2ml/100ml OXYGEN CONCENTRATION
DURING EXERCISE

Long-term effects of training on the circulatory system with regular aerobic endurance training

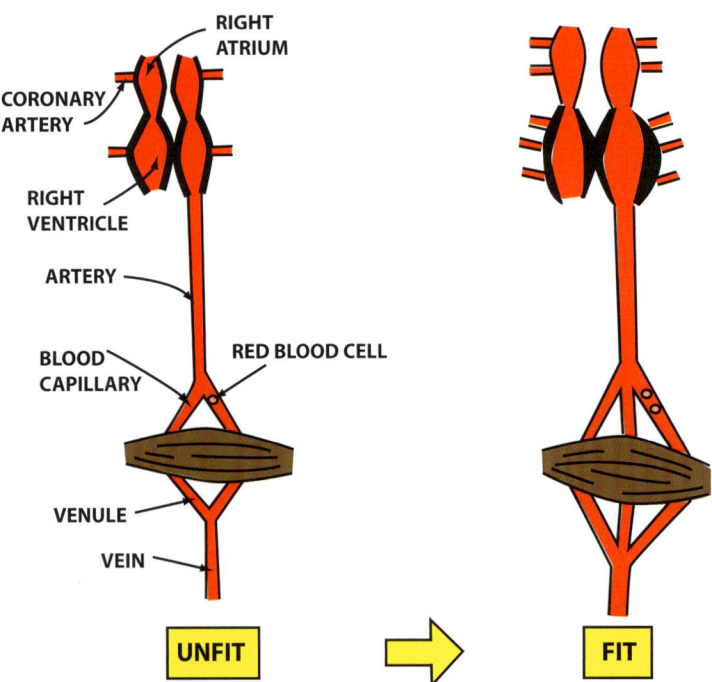

The heart develops more **coronary arteries**. This means it can get a greater supply of blood bringing oxygen and nutrients and so can work harder and more efficiently.

The stroke volume of the heart improves. The heart becomes larger with thicker and stronger muscular walls. This means the chambers can be emptied more fully on each contraction. The heart chambers also become larger, and can therefore hold more blood for each contraction.

The arteries become larger and more elastic. This makes them more efficient in carrying the increased blood supply during exercise.

More blood capillaries develop in the muscles. This means they get a greater supply of blood bringing oxygen and nutrients, and with more venules they are more able to get rid of waste products.

More red blood cells are produced in the large bones of the body. This means more oxygen can be carried by the blood.

All this means that for the same number of heart beats, you are able to have a higher work rate than before and to keep going for longer than before.

Musculatory system

Muscles produce movement:

- **Skeletal muscle** moves limbs, for example the **biceps**.
- **Cardiac muscle** moves blood through the body, for example the heart.
- **Smooth muscle** moves food through the digestive system, for example the small intestine.

Main skeletal muscles

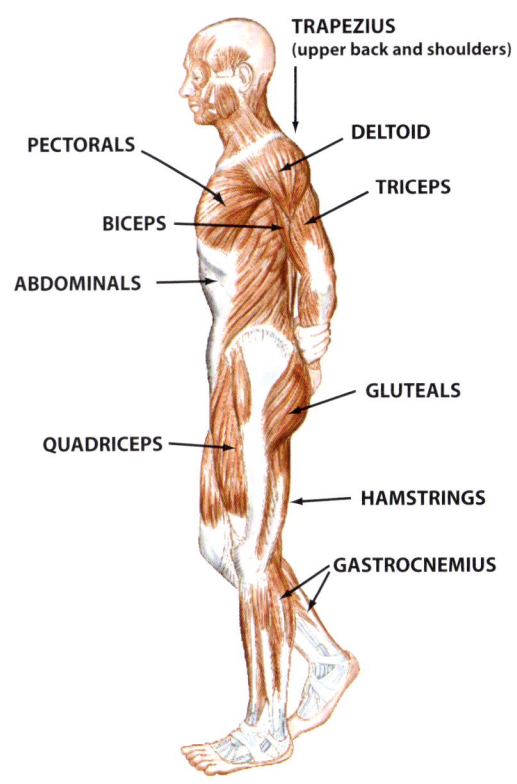

TRAPEZIUS
(upper back and shoulders)

DELTOID

PECTORALS

TRICEPS

BICEPS

ABDOMINALS

GLUTEALS

QUADRICEPS

HAMSTRINGS

GASTROCNEMIUS

Terms used to describe skeletal muscles working

Muscles work in pairs. The two muscles which work together are known as an **antagonistic pair**. When one is the prime mover the other is the antagonist.

Flexor muscle bends a limb, while **extensor muscle** straightens a limb – for example biceps/ triceps.

Isometric contraction involves no movement of body parts. **Isotonic contraction** involves movement of body parts.

Concentric contraction involves the muscle getting shorter and fatter. **Eccentric contraction** involves the muscle getting longer and thinner.

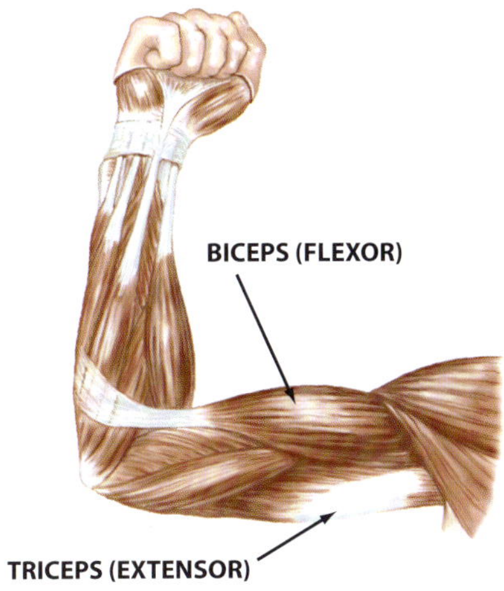

BICEPS (FLEXOR)

TRICEPS (EXTENSOR)

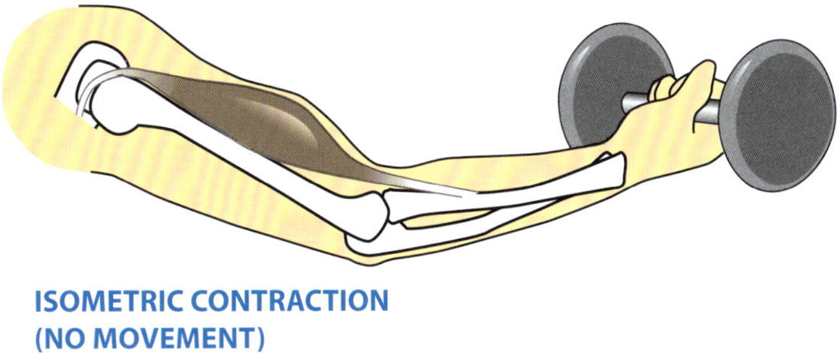

ISOMETRIC CONTRACTION
(NO MOVEMENT)

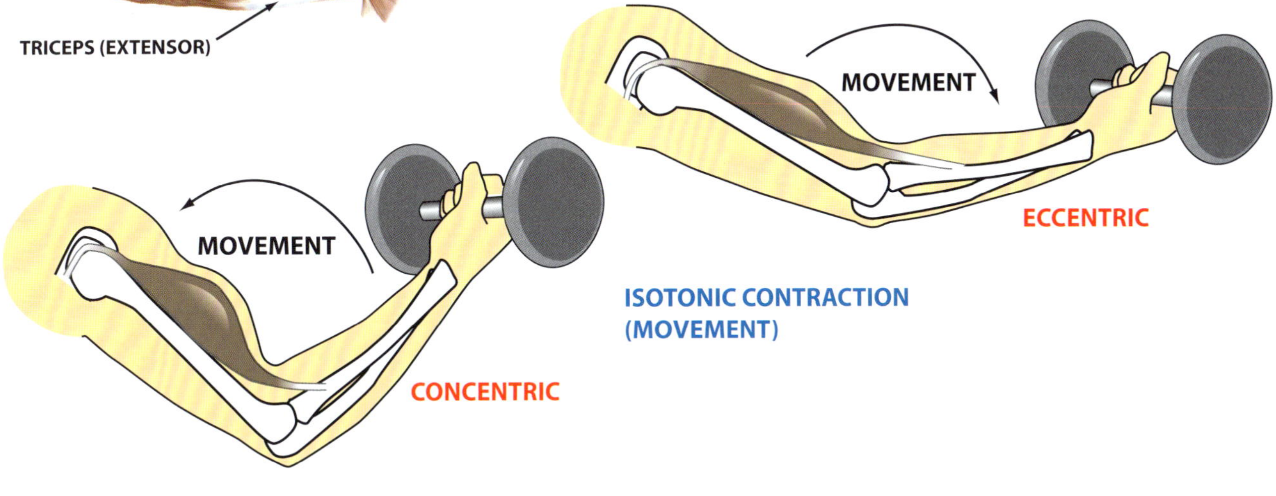

MOVEMENT

ECCENTRIC

ISOTONIC CONTRACTION
(MOVEMENT)

MOVEMENT

CONCENTRIC

73

Factors influencing performance

Ratio of fast twitch muscle fibres to slow twitch muscle fibres

Fast twitch and **slow twitch** are two types of skeletal muscle fibres.

Fast twitch contract quickly and relax quickly, while slow twitch contract slowly and relax slowly. Fast twitch contract and relax three times more quickly than slow twitch.

Fast twitch produce much force, while slow twitch produce little force. Fast twitch produce ten times more force than slow twitch.

Fast twitch tire quickly, while slow twitch keep going for long periods without tiring. This is because slow twitch have more arteries and veins than fast twitch and three times the amount of **myoglobin**. It is myoglobin that brings the oxygen carried in the blood into the muscle cells. Slow twitch also have bigger and 12 times more **mitochondria** than fast twitch. The mitochondria in the muscle cells are like factories that burn the fuel with the oxygen in order to create energy.

The ratio of fast twitch to slow twitch muscle fibres is controlled genetically. People with high proportions of fast twitch muscle fibres should do well in activities which don't last very long but demand speed, strength or power, for example sprinting and shot put. People with high proportions of slow twitch muscle fibres should do well in activities which last for long periods of time but demand relatively little speed, strength or power, for example 5,000m or marathon.

Control of muscle actions

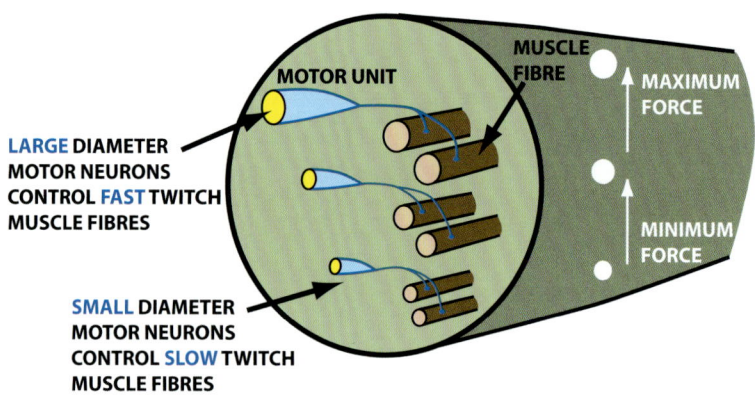

Skeletal muscles are controlled by the **central nervous system (CNS)**.

To increase muscle force, the **motor neurons** are brought into play one by one, smallest to the largest. Small diameter motor neurons are used for actions that require little force. If the force required increases then larger and larger motor neurons are used.

Muscle tone is the ability of the muscles to hold a position.

Short-term or immediate effects of exercise on the skeletal muscles

Muscles need **ATP (adenosine triphosphate)** as a fuel to produce energy.

The ATP is supplied to the muscle by three systems:

- the **alactic anaerobic system**
- the **lactic acid anaerobic system**
- the **aerobic energy system**

Anaerobic energy production

To produce energy for very high-intensity work, the alactic system first uses the stores of ATP in the muscles. This produces energy for approximately one second. After this, stores of **creatine phosphate** are broken down to provide ATP. This source of fuel produces approximately another nine seconds of energy. The alactic system produces this energy without needing oxygen.

Beyond 10 seconds of high-intensity work it is the lactic acid system that supplies the ATP. **Glycogen** (what our carbohydrate food becomes after digestion) is broken down to form ATP. The stores of glycogen can provide energy for up to 40 seconds before the build-up of the waste product of lactic acid stops the muscles from working. The alactic and lactic acid systems provide fuel for high-intensity work when the respiratory and circulatory systems are unable to meet the muscles' demands for oxygen. In total this can be for up to 50 seconds.

For a short burst of very high-intensity work (for example, a 5 to 10 second sprint or shot put) the main energy system used will be the alactic energy system.

For a long burst of very high-intensity work (for example, a 30 to 50 second sprint) the main energy system used will be the lactic acid energy system.

As the fuel sources for anaerobic energy production are used up the muscles become tired, painful and eventually stop working altogether.

After very strenuous exercise it is important to replace the fuel sources and to get rid of waste products such as lactic acid. This requires oxygen in substantial quantities – hence the need for fast and deep breathing, and for the stroke volume and heart rate to remain high to carry lots of oxygen to the muscles during recovery. This need to replace the fuel sources and to remove lactic acid is known as the **oxygen debt**. During your recovery you are said to be paying back the oxygen debt.

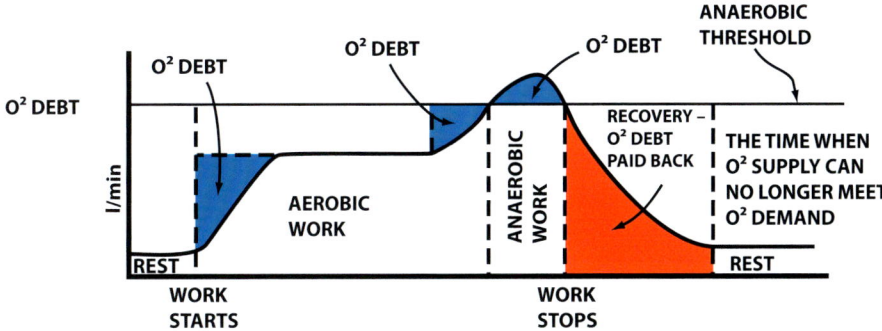

Aerobic energy production

The aerobic energy system is used when the exercise is not as intense and the respiratory and circulatory systems are able to deliver sufficient oxygen to the working muscles. Glycogen and fats are broken down to provide ATP. The waste products created from producing the energy are broken down by using oxygen and can be breathed out as carbon dioxide. You can keep going using the aerobic energy system until you run out of glycogen.

For a long time at moderate-intensity work (for example, jogging or running for 20 minutes) the main energy system used will be the aerobic energy system.

The proportion of energy produced by each of the three systems depends on the intensity and duration of the exercise. The graph on the next page shows the relationship between running time and the contribution of the different energy systems.

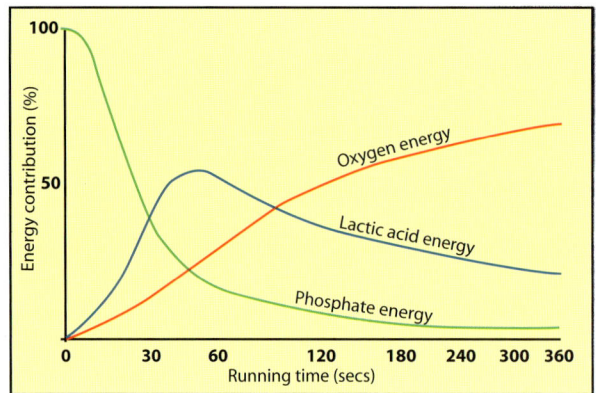

The following information shows when each energy system is dominant in a 5,000m race:

- First 10 seconds – the alactic energy system is predominant.

- 10–20 seconds – there is a transition from the alactic to the lactic acid energy system.

- 20 seconds to 2 minutes – the lactic acid energy system is predominant.

- 2–5 minutes – there is a transition from the lactic acid energy system to the aerobic energy system.

- 5 minutes plus – the aerobic energy system is predominant.

- Final 30-second sprint – the lactic acid system is predominant.

When energy is produced, heat is created so the muscles become warm.

Long-term effects of training on the skeletal muscles

As a result of regular aerobic endurance training, the slow twitch muscle fibres get:

- an increased network of arteries, capillaries and veins. This means more oxygen and nutrients (food) can be delivered to the muscles and more waste products (carbon dioxide and water) can be taken away.

- increased stores of myoglobin. This means up to 80% more oxygen can be taken into the muscle.

- an increase in the number and size of mitochondria. This means the muscle can produce more energy.

All of these effects mean that you can perform better aerobically. You can work harder and for longer than before.

As a result of regular strength training, the fast twitch muscle fibres get:

- an increased cross-sectional area (the diameter increases). This means the muscle can produce more force.

- increased stores of high-energy phosphagens. This means the muscles can work at a high intensity for longer.

These effects mean you perform better because you can produce more force and can work longer at very high intensity.

Skeletal system

The skeleton:

- provides protection. For example, the skull protects the brain, and the rib cage protects the heart and lungs.
- allows movement. It is jointed to allow us a wide range of movement.
- provides a rigid structure for the attachment of the muscles. The muscles pull on the bones and produce movement.
- helps produce the blood cells in the larger bones of the body.
- stores calcium. Calcium can be temporarily absorbed from the bones if our diet does not supply sufficient calcium for our needs.

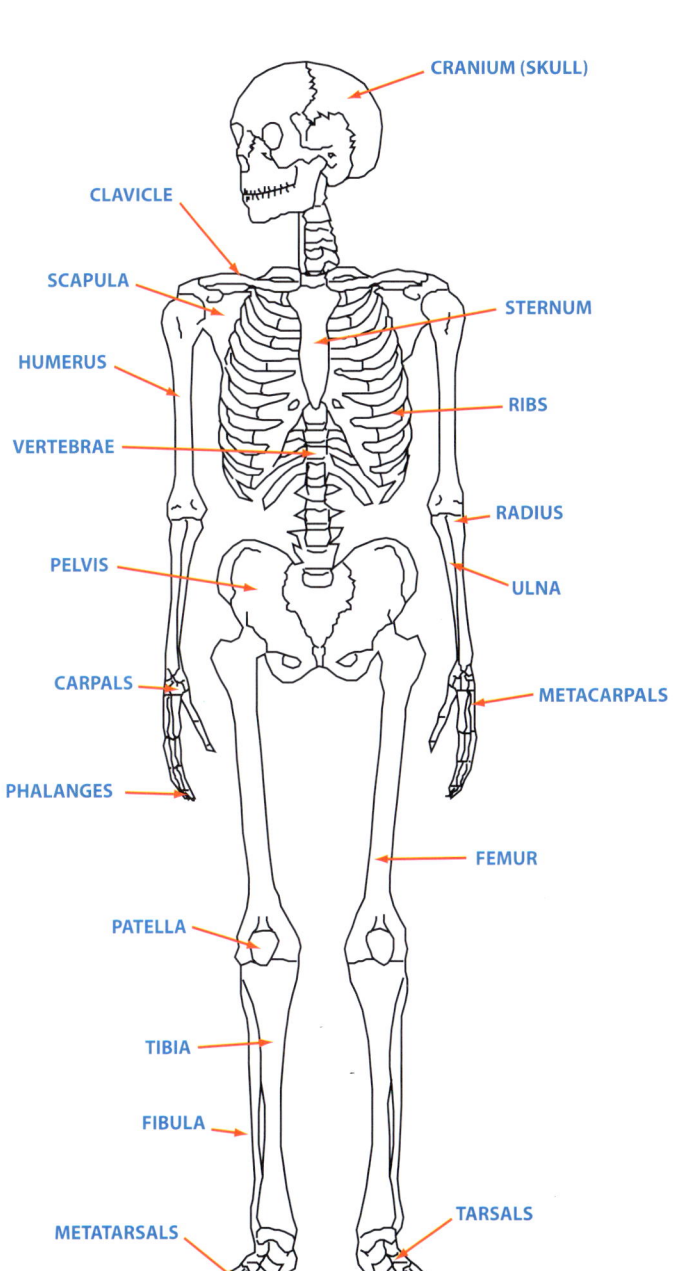

Main parts of the skeleton

There are 206 bones.

The **axial skeleton**: skull, spine (vertebrae), rib cage (ribs, sternum)

The **appendicular skeleton**: shoulder girdle (clavicle, scapula), arms (humerus, radius, ulna, carpals, metacarpals, phalanges), pelvic girdle, legs (femur, tibia, fibula, patella, tarsals, metatarsals, phalanges)

Types of joints

A joint is a place where two or more bones meet. There are three main types of joint:

- **fibrous**
- **cartilaginous**
- **synovial**

Moveable joints are called **synovial joints**.

The synovial joint

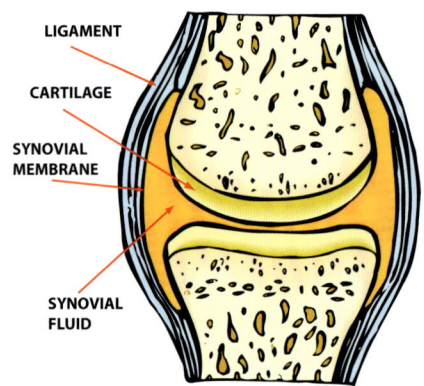

Ligaments hold the bones in place.

Cartilage acts as a shock absorber and is smooth and slippery (friction-free movement).

The joint is surrounded by a **synovial membrane** which produces **synovial fluid**. The synovial fluid oils the joint, keeping it moist and working smoothly.

Types of synovial joints

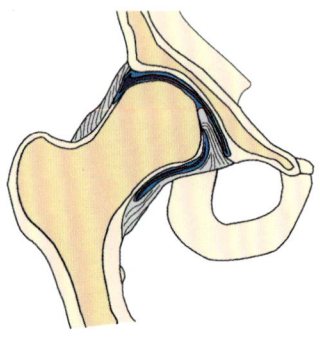

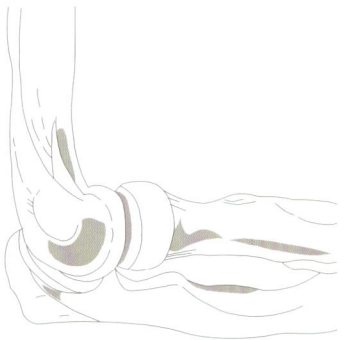
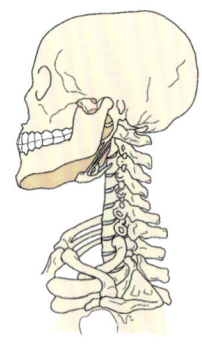
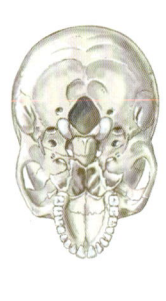

Ball and socket: hip (all directions)

Hinge: elbow (bend and straighten)

Pivot: neck/head (rotation)

Factors influencing performance

There are three aspects of the skeleton which can influence performance:

● the skeleton's overall size. Consider the requirements of basketball and shot put compared to gymnastics and trampolining.

● the skeleton's proportions. For example, good runners have long legs in proportion to their upper bodies, and good alpine skiers have long upper bodies in proportion to their legs.

● the size of parts of the skeleton. For example, a narrow pelvis (sprinting), long arms (boxing), big hands and feet (swimming), and big chest (rowing, cross-country skiing).

These factors are genetically controlled.

Short-term or immediate effects of exercise on the skeleton

Mobility exercises, flexibility exercises and pulse-raising exercises 'loosen up' the joints. The synovial fluid is warmed and becomes less sticky (viscous), allowing greater ease of movement. The ligaments and muscles surrounding the joint become more flexible and so a greater range of movement is possible.

Long-term effects of training on the skeleton

With regular and appropriate training the bones become thicker and have a greater mineral content, so they are kept strong. The joints are also kept flexible.

However, too much training, training which is too intense, or too much training on hard surfaces can cause overuse injuries. Cartilage is worn away, and **stress fractures** and **tendon injuries** occur.

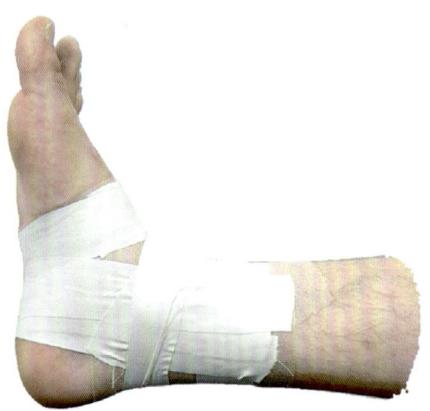

Digestive system

The digestive system breaks down the food we eat into smaller and smaller pieces (**digestion**). When these pieces are small enough they pass through the intestine wall and dissolve in the blood (**absorption**).

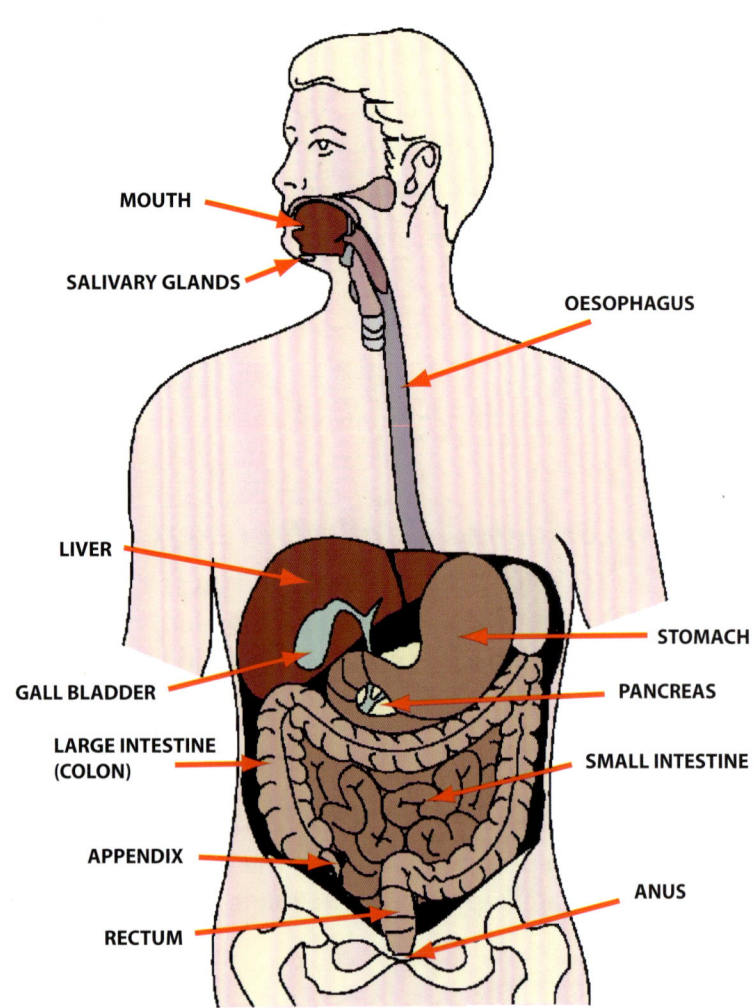

MOUTH

SALIVARY GLANDS

OESOPHAGUS

LIVER

STOMACH

GALL BLADDER

PANCREAS

LARGE INTESTINE (COLON)

SMALL INTESTINE

APPENDIX

ANUS

RECTUM

Main parts of the digestive system

How digestion works

Digestion is brought about in two ways:

- mechanically – by the teeth, tongue and the muscles in the walls of the alimentary canal
- chemically – by the enzymes and other chemicals made by the salivary glands, liver and pancreas

Foods are broken down into the following:

- Carbohydrates are broken down into simple sugars like **glucose**.
- Proteins are broken down into **amino acids**.
- Fats are broken down into fatty acids and **glycerol**.
- Minerals, vitamins and water are released from their packaging.

Short-term or immediate effects of exercise on the digestive system

During exercise, digestion effectively stops as blood flow is largely diverted to the muscles. At rest the gut gets 25–30% of the blood flow, but during exercise it gets less than 5% (see page 71).

This helps explain why you should eat at least two hours in advance of taking part in vigorous exercise and why this pre-exercise meal should consist mainly of carbohydrates. Carbohydrates are digested quicker than fats and protein so you are more likely to have digested your meal and therefore have the energy from it available for your vigorous exercise. If you eat a meal of fat and protein, or eat any food not long before your vigorous exercise, it is likely that this food will still be in your digestive system when you start to exercise. As the digestive system effectively closes down during vigorous exercise, the energy from this food will not be available to you and you will carry this food around with you as you exercise. This can be uncomfortable and affect your performance.

TASK 1 on Effects

Purpose

To understand the positioning of the body systems in relation to each other and to understand the short-term effects of exercise on each.

Instructions

On an outline of the human body use simple drawings to show the positioning of the main parts of the following body systems: the respiratory system, the circulatory system, the musculatory system, the skeletal system, and the digestive system.

Label your diagrams to show the short-term or immediate effects of exercise on each of the body systems.

Task 2 on Effects

Purpose

To understand the positioning of the body systems in relation to each other and to understand the long-term effects of exercise on each.

Instructions

On an outline of the human body use simple drawings to show the positioning of the main parts of the following body systems: the respiratory system, the circulatory system, the musculatory system, and the skeletal system.

Label your diagrams to show the long-term effects that appropriate exercise has on each of the body systems.

SUMMARY

In this section you have learnt the main functions of the respiratory, circulatory, musculatory, skeletal and digestive systems and how they work and respond when you start to exercise.

Most importantly, you have learnt what physical changes take place in the body systems as a result of regular and appropriate exercise/training and how these physical changes make the systems more efficient.

This increased efficiency accounts for you becoming fitter and performing better than before.

Section 8

Genetic factors

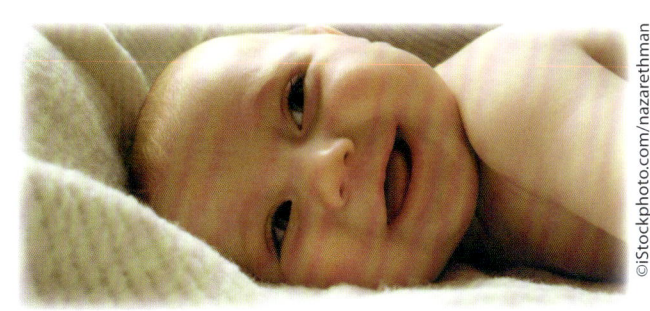

©iStockphoto.com/nazarethman

Genetic type factors that affect the development of physical health/wellbeing, peak physical fitness, and skilled performance

In Section 2 you learnt how diet, drugs, tobacco, alcohol, rest/ sleep and exercise can affect the development of physical health/ wellbeing, peak physical fitness and skilled performance.

These are factors from lifestyle over which you have control. In this section you will consider the effects of the following **genetic type factors,** over which you have no or limited control:

- age
- gender
- height
- weight
- body proportions
- body type
- ratio of fast twitch muscle fibres to slow twitch muscle fibres
- vital capacity
- stroke volume

The lifestyle factors studied in Section 2 influence your *actual* physical wellbeing, physical fitness and skilled performance at a particular time. 'Actual' in this context means the reality of the effects of these factors at a particular time.

The genetic type factors considered in this section influence your *potential* to be successful in physical activities. 'Potential' in this context means your upper limit or the best that you could possibly be.

Age

During childhood your body systems are still developing and therefore your potential to perform well in physical tasks will be lower than during the time of maturity. In old age the body systems are deteriorating and so your potential to perform well in physical tasks will again be lower than during the time of maturity.

After birth, the **first year** is a period of fast growth when height and weight increase rapidly. As the nervous system and muscles develop, babies are able to lift their heads, sit up, crawl, stand and eventually walk.

After the first year and up to puberty, there is a period of steady growth in height and weight. The nervous system and muscles continue to develop and children become able, with practice, to run, jump, hop, kick, catch and throw.

Puberty is a period of rapid growth and development. There is a rapid increase in height and weight. In the female, the breasts enlarge and there is an increase of body fat on the thighs and hips. In the male, the shoulders broaden and there is an increase in muscle bulk.

During puberty most males and females benefit from the physical changes that occur, but this is not always the case. For example, due to the physical changes females may not perform as well in activities such as gymnastics. Also, during puberty the limbs might grow very fast and teenagers get taller before their muscles have developed to match the growth spurt – for a while they might feel gangly and awkward.

After puberty there is a time of **maturity**. The body systems have fully developed and your potential is at its highest. Your physical fitness can be developed to what will be its highest peak and you can be at your most skilled in performances.

As you **age** the body systems deteriorate and become less efficient. For example:

- Muscles shrivel and muscle reflexes diminish.

- There is a loss of elasticity of the aorta and weakening of the heart muscle cells. Heart output is reduced. Arteries narrow, raising blood pressure and reducing the brain's blood supply.

- The lung tissue of the alveoli and the bronchioles lose their elasticity and become less inflatable.

- Nerve cells die each day and the brain slowly shrinks. Both reflex and voluntary movements become slower and the sense of balance becomes poor.

- Joints wear out as the joint cartilages deteriorate. Joint surfaces become rough and irregular. Bone becomes brittle as it gradually loses its collagen framework and hence its ability to hold calcium.

- Eyes lose their range of focus and may develop cataracts (cloudy lenses) or glaucoma (excessive pressure in the eyeball). Hearing becomes dimmer.

These changes reduce your potential to perform well.

©iStockphoto.com/duncan1890

 Gender

Your gender can influence your potential performance.

There is little difference between the genders during childhood. However, the physical differences between the genders, as a result of puberty, favour the male in physical activities. It can be argued that the mature female is at a disadvantage against the mature male because of her shorter stature, different bone structure, lower body weight, less muscle, more fat, smaller heart and lungs, less blood volume, and less haemoglobin in the blood. This is one factor that helps to explain why in many physical sports males compete against males and females compete against females, ensuring physical equality between competitors.

Height, weight and body type

Height is usually measured in centimetres or feet and inches. Being tall can help you to be successful in sports like basketball. Being small can be an advantage in sports like artistic gymnastics.

Weight is usually measured in kilograms or stones and pounds. Being heavy is not necessarily about having lots of fat. Some people are heavier than others because they have big frames and heavy bones. Being heavy can be of benefit for certain positions in rugby. Being light can help you to be successful in sports such as horse racing. In many sports where weight would be an advantage, the governing bodies set weight categories so that those of similar weights compete against each other – for example boxing and judo.

Body type describes your shape and build. There are three extremes in body type – **endomorph**, **mesomorph** and **ectomorph**. Extreme endomorphs are pear-shaped with their hips being broader than their shoulders, and they have lots of body fat. Extreme mesomorphs are triangular-shaped with broad shoulders and narrow waists, and they have lots of muscle. Extreme ectomorphs are linear in shape with narrow shoulders and narrow hips, and they have little muscle and little fat.

Body type is measured on a scale from one to seven for each of the three extremes, with the scores being given in the following order – endomorph score first (1–7), mesomorph score second (1–7) and ectomorph score third (1–7). An extreme endomorph's score would be 7:1:1. An extreme mesomorph's score would be 1:7:1. An extreme ectomorph's score would be 1:1:7.

There may be an ideal height, weight and body type for each sport, or position within a sport. It may therefore be possible to use these factors to indicate if a person has the potential to be successful in a particular sport, by analysing the requirements of that sport .

The requirements of gymnastics mean that successful gymnasts tend to be small and reasonably light. They also tend towards mesomorphy in body type (rating 1:7:2). In other words they are triangular-shaped. They have little fat on their body and have lots of highly-defined muscle.

The requirements of high jump mean that successful high jumpers tend to be tall and light. They also tend towards ectomorphy in body type (rating 1:3:7). In other words they are linear in shape. They have little fat and don't usually have highly-defined muscles.

©iStockphoto.com/pomortzeff

The requirements of field events (shot put, discus, hammer) mean successful field athletes tend to be tall and heavy. They tend towards endomorphy/mesomorphy in body type (rating 4:7:1). In other words they may have noticeable fat on their body, but they also have lots of muscle. They would be more triangular-shaped than pear-shaped or have both broad shoulders and hips.

◯ Body proportions

The size of body parts in relation to other body parts or in relation to other people's body parts can have an influence on potential. For example, having big hands can help in swimming as the hands act as paddles. Having big feet again can help in swimming as the feet act as flippers. Having long arms can help in sports like boxing where you have an advantage in reach over your opponents, or in field events like discus where greater leverage is gained by having long arms. Having long legs in relation to the length of the body can help in running events, and having short legs in relation to the length of the body can help in sports such as skiing.

Although height, weight, body type and body proportions can help identify possible potential for sports or events, they cannot determine the efficiency of the body systems involved in performance. This can be even more important in influencing potential performance.

◯ Ratio of fast twitch muscle fibres compared to slow twitch muscle fibres

See Section 7, page 75, for information on this.

◯ Vital capacity

See Section 7, page 69, for more information on this.

With a greater vital capacity more oxygen can be taken into the blood from the lungs and transported to the muscles. People with a high vital capacity have greater potential to perform well in aerobic endurance activities like the 5,000m or 10,000m running events.

◯ Stroke volume

Stroke volume is the amount of blood pumped out from the heart (left ventricle) in each beat. Cardiac output is the amount of blood pumped out from the left side of the heart in one minute. With a greater stroke volume and cardiac output more blood, and therefore more oxygen and nutrients, can be pumped to the muscles. People with a high stroke volume have greater potential to perform well in aerobic endurance activities like the 5,000m or 10,000m running events.

▷ TASK on Genetic factors

Purpose

To analyse the requirements of events or sports and describe the physical characteristics that would indicate potential to be successful in these events or sports.

Instructions

From the genetic type factors discussed in this section, describe the likely characteristics that would indicate potential to be world-record holders in the following physical activities:

- competition weight-lifting
- marathon running
- 25m sprint swimming

◯ SUMMARY

Stu Forster/Getty Images

Your age, gender, height, lean weight, body type, body proportions, ratio of fast twitch muscle fibres to slow twitch muscle fibres, vital capacity and stroke volume are factors over which you have limited control. However, they can influence your potential physical fitness and your potential to perform successfully in events and sports.

In the next section you will look at factors that can affect your health and safety when exercising or training.

Tony Duffy/Getty Images

Section 9

Health & safety

©iStockphoto.com/Hohenhaus

Health and safety in participation and performance in physical activities

In previous sections you have learnt how exercise should be used to keep you fit and healthy, and the effects this exercise has on the body. In this section you will learn about exercising safely.

A **hazard** is something that can cause illness, injury or even death. You need to be able to identify potential hazards in the context of exercising. The following are examples of potential hazards:

- exercising when you are already ill or injured
- going over the top in following an exercise programme that is not appropriate for you
- not eating, eating the wrong foods, or eating at the wrong times
- wearing inappropriate clothing or footwear
- exercising on a wet and slippy floor
- not warming up, not using equipment properly, not following the rules, and not using sound techniques

Regular exercise is good for your health. However, if it is done thoughtlessly it can become a hazard and cause ill health. Safety must be a priority when you exercise. By identifying potential hazards you can take steps to minimise the risk of illness or injury occurring. Remember, prevention should always be your priority.

Present health

Most people do not need a medical examination before taking exercise. However, if you have chest problems (such as asthma or bronchitis), heart disease, high blood pressure, joint pains, a serious illness, or you are recovering from an operation, you should consult your doctor about the best form of exercise for you.

If you are suffering from a viral infection (such as the flu) then you shouldn't exercise until you have recovered.

If you have an injury which a particular type of exercise would make worse or would slow the recovery of, then you should get treatment and find an alternative type of exercise, or stop exercising altogether until the injury has gone.

When exercising, you should stop if you feel pain, or feel dizzy, unusually tired, or sick. If the symptoms do not go away, or come back later, or you are worried about them then go and see your doctor.

Drugs

If you are on a course of drugs for medical reasons you should check whether it is safe or advisable to exercise while taking them.

If you are serious about your health you will avoid such habits as cigarette-smoking and excessive consumption of alcohol.

You will also stay clear of drugs such as heroin and cocaine, as they have only negative effects on your health.

You should avoid the temptation to take body-building drugs such as anabolic steroids, or other performance-enhancing drugs as they can have serious side effects.

The exercise/training programme

Exercise/training programmes should begin gently and build up gently and gradually. They should apply the principles of training (see Section 5) sensibly according to each individual's situation. Your personal exercise programme should consider factors such as your age, gender, body type, present level of fitness, your personal choice of exercise, time available, money available, and facilities and amenities available.

Your personal exercise/training programme should also be SMART – Specific, Measurable, Attainable, Realistic, and Tenable.

Eating and drinking

Meals should generally have a high percentage of carbohydrate compared to fat and protein – for example 60% carbohydrate, 25% fat, and 15% protein. This keeps the fuel tanks in the muscles and liver topped up and therefore allows the body to perform more efficiently.

You should not exercise immediately after a meal, but should wait, if possible, two hours before exercising. You should eat as soon as possible after exercising to restore the fuel reserves that were used.

Generally you should drink lots of liquids, for example water. If exercise is to last more than 30 minutes you should drink small quantities of liquids during it, on a regular basis. This is particularly important in hot conditions.

Clothing and footwear

The principles to be followed are to protect the body and to allow freedom of movement.

- Footwear should fit properly and should provide support, protection, grip and shock absorption. Socks should fit properly.
- Inner clothing should absorb sweat and take it away from the body.

- In hot conditions little clothing should be worn. What is worn should protect you from the sun, yet allow good circulation of air.

- In cold, wet or other hostile conditions sufficient clothing must be worn to protect you, yet allow you freedom of movement. The colder it is the more important it is to protect the body, head and limbs. This is generally done by using layers of clothing combined with a waterproof yet breathable outer garment.

The environment

You should aim to exercise in a safe environment which minimises the risk of injury. Consider the surface on which you exercise, for example:

- running on pavements compared to running on grass;

- the pollution level of the air or water in which you exercise, for example running during the rush-hour traffic compared to running in the park;

- the temperature of the air or water in which you exercise, for example, swimming in the sea in winter compared to in a swimming pool.

When exercising indoors you should consider the space, ventilation, lighting, heating and floor surface of the area.

Equipment

When equipment is necessary for exercising you should ensure that it is safe and in good working condition. It should also be used properly. For example, if you go to a gym, weights should be properly secured on barbells and dumbbells, weight-lifting and aerobic machines should be working properly and you should use them as directed.

If you are involved in sports where equipment is available to minimise the risks of injury then you should use it. For example, you should wear gum shields for hockey and rugby, shin pads for football and hockey, and helmets for cricket and hurling.

Have proper landing areas for high jump, and cages for discus and hammer, and so on.

Warm-up and cool-down

Warm-up prepares the body for the workout so that you are less likely to pull or tear muscles. Cool-down leaves the body in the best possible condition before exercise stops. It slowly brings everything back to normal.

Techniques

This refers to the sequence of movements required to perform skills. You should learn and use the proper techniques as you are then less likely to get injured.

Rules

Many rules of activities are there to protect and thus prevent injury to the participants. You should play by the rules of the game and in the spirit of the game.

TASK on Health & safety

Purpose

To help you to critically analyse situations to identify potential hazards, then to suggest precautions that would help minimise the risks.

Instructions

For each of the following situations identify the potential hazards and then explain how the risks associated with these hazards could be minimised

Situation 1

A person lives and works in a large city. They wish to cycle to and from work over the winter months.

Situation 2

A person joins a large gym. They want to do weight training, which is new to them, to build up their muscle strength.

SUMMARY

In this section you studied how your present health, drugs, an exercise/training programme, your eating and drinking habits, your clothing and footwear, the environment, the equipment used, a warm-up and cool-down, your techniques, and the rules of sport can affect your health and safety when exercising/training.

Exercising should be about good health and fitness rather than illness and injury. It is therefore important that you can identify potential hazards associated with the factors covered, and that you are able to take steps to minimise the risks from these hazards. By doing this you are more likely to remain healthy and physically fit, and to perform well in sport.

In the next section the focus will change from developing physical fitness to developing skilled performances.

Section 10
Skilled performance

Your level of physical fitness is a major factor that can determine how well you perform in physical activities or sport. Your range of skills and your mastery of them is another major factor. In this section you will look at skill and how you can become skilled.

◯ Skilled performance

Skilled performance or **skill** is the learnt ability to bring about a predetermined goal or result with maximum certainty and efficiency.

> Sparrow and Newell (1998) defined skill as "the ability to economically coordinate and control the movement to achieve the task goal."

When you carry out a physical task then that can be described as a performance.

In physical education and sport we are often concerned with how well a task or performance is done.

In observing skilled performance you will be aware that the person has an outcome that he or she wishes to achieve. It may be making a pass in netball, scoring a goal in football, or sinking a putt in golf, but in performing a skill there will be an outcome to be achieved.

In observing skilled performance or a skill the skill or action will be carried out **effectively** and **efficiently** – the pass in netball will go to the intended player at the right height and with the correct pace, the football will go into the goal beyond the reach of the goalkeeper, and the golf ball will follow the lie of the green and have the right pace to drop into the hole. In other words the skill will have been performed effectively. These actions or skills will all be made to look easy, with minimum effort being used to perform them. In other words the skills will have been performed efficiently.

In observing skilled performance the skill or action will be carried out effectively and efficiently time after time, with few mistakes being made – that is, with **consistency**. The person will be consistently successful.

Skills are learnt. The person may make the performance look easy and natural but he or she will have gone through the stages of learning a skill like everyone else. He or she will have had **feedback** on performances and spent hours **practising** to get to the final stage where they can perform the skill automatically without having to think about it.

Skilled performance for an individual is **relative**, depending on the context. A person may be skilled in one sport but not in another, and even within a sport a person can be at various stages of learning in the mastery of the skills of that sport. For example, in badminton a person could be skilled in performing a forehand overhead clear but not in performing a backhand overhead clear.

There are endless skills that you have learnt and can perform automatically. From an early age you start learning skills such as hopping, jumping, and reading and writing. You learn to ride a bike, to swim, to knit, to sew, and to cook. You learn skills from sports, etc. There are so many different skills that people try to classify them.

You should be aware of the following classifications.

The basic to complex continuum

Jumping

Back somersault with a full twist

Basic ———————————————————————— **Complex**

Jamie Squire/Getty Images

Skills can be classified at one extreme as being **basic skills** and at the other extreme as being **complex skills**, or they can be placed somewhere in between these two extremes.

The simpler the skill and the less there is involved in learning it the more likely it will be placed towards the basic end of the continuum. The more complicated the skill and the more there is involved in learning it the more likely it will be placed towards the complex end of the continuum.

A skill such as hopping or jumping would be considered as being a basic skill whereas a back somersault with a full twist on the trampoline would be considered a complex skill.

The closed to open continuum

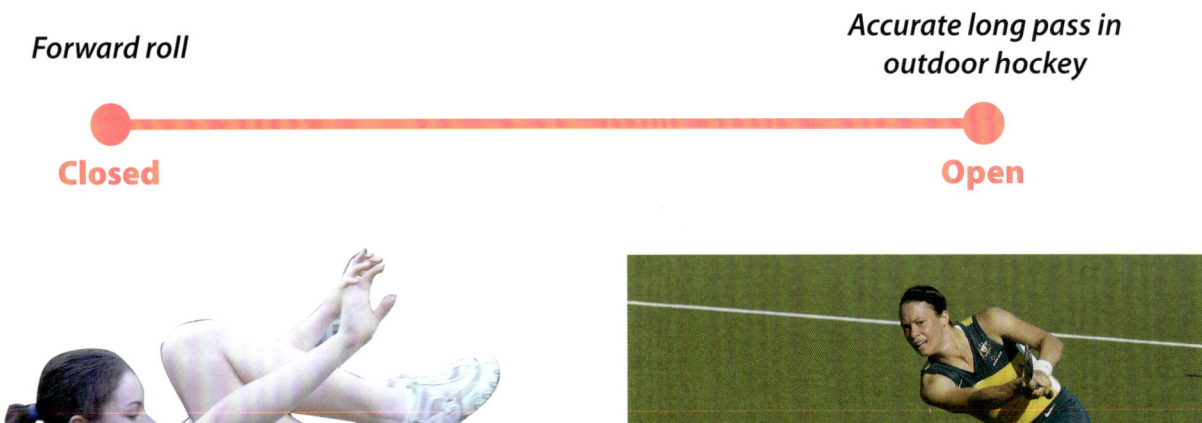

Forward roll

Accurate long pass in outdoor hockey

Closed

Open

Clive Mason/Getty Images

Skills can be classified at one extreme as being **closed skills** and at the other extreme as being **open skills**, or they can be placed somewhere in between these two extremes.

The fewer the number of factors outside the control of the performer and the less that these factors impact on the performance of the skill, the more likely the skill will be placed towards the closed end of the continuum.

The greater the number of factors outside the control of the performer and the more that these factors impact on the performance of the skill, the more likely the skill will be placed towards the open end of the continuum.

A skill such as a forward roll performed on a mat on a gym floor would be considered as being a closed skill, whereas providing a quality long pass to a team-mate in an outdoor game such as hockey would be considered as being an open skill.

Finally, skills can be classified as **discrete**, **continuous** or **serial** skills.

A discrete skill has a definite start and finish. It can stand alone. For example, doing a forward roll on a mat is a discrete skill.

A continuous skill is repeated over and over again. For example, rowing is a continuous skill.

A serial skill is a number of skills that have been linked together, for example performing a tumbling routine on the floor in gymnastics.

©iStockphoto.com/barsik

Cognitive, perceptual, motor, and perceptual motor skills

Cognitive skills are those that involve the brain working, for example, reading instructions over and over again to learn how to serve in badminton.

Perceptual skills are those that involve the brain having to interpret given information and to make decisions based on it. For example, in badminton you look at where your opponent is standing in the service court and then you decide which area of the court you will serve to.

Motor skills are those that involve the control of the muscles in carrying out movements. For example, being able to hit the shuttlecock to the area of the service court that you intended involves the brain telling the muscles the sequence of movements you want. In sports such as gymnastics and trampolining the main focus is on the successful execution of motor skills.

Perceptual motor skills involve all of the above – the thinking, the interpretation and the execution of movements. In net games such as badminton and tennis and in invasion games such as hockey and basketball you need to know how to do things (cognitive), you need to be able to read situations in the game and to make the right decisions for those situations (perceptual), and you need to be able to execute the skills efficiently and effectively for your decisions to be carried out successfully (motor).

Coordination, balance, reaction time and agility

To learn a motor skill you need to know the **technique** of the skill. The technique is the sequence of movements that are carried out to perform the skill efficiently and effectively. Techniques are the building blocks of skilled performance. Underpinning how well you perform the techniques of skills are coordination, balance, reaction time and agility.

Coordination is the ability of the brain and muscles to work together to perform smooth, accurate movements. It is about getting the timing of the sequence of movements right (the techniques). If you can consistently do this then you are more likely to be regarded as being skilled. If the timing is slightly late in playing a smash shot in badminton it can mean the shuttlecock is smashed onto your side of the court; similarly, if the timing is slightly early it can mean that the shuttle hits the ceiling or goes high but lands mid-court on your opponent's side.

Balance is the ability to be in a state of **equilibrium** (stable, not falling over), whether static or moving. Balance is about being in a position to be able to perform the sequence of movements of a skill under control. If you can consistently provide a base to allow this to happen then you are more likely to be regarded as being skilled. If you are off balance in trying to play a smash shot in badminton it may be impossible for you to go through the full sequence of movements and the shot will not be effective, or the timing can be affected by you being rushed to take the shot.

Reaction time is your ability to react to a **stimulus**. It is the time that lapses from the presentation of the stimulus to the start of your response – for example the time it takes for you to react to the starting pistol at the start of a 100m sprint, or to react to your opponent's shot in a game of badminton. If you are consistently quick to react in an appropriate way then you are more likely to be regarded as being skilled. The longer it takes for you to react to the opponent's shots in a game of badminton the less time you have to move towards the shuttlecock, get balanced, and play an effective return shot.

Agility is the ability to change direction efficiently and effectively when moving at speed. It is about being able to stop, start, or to change from going forwards to backwards or to sideways quickly and with control. If you are consistently good at this then you are more likely to be regarded as being skilled. If you are slow to move, to stop or to change direction quickly in a game of badminton, you will often not be able to get into balanced positions to play your opponent's shots.

Assessment of coordination, balance, reaction time and agility

Coordination, balance, reaction time and agility underpin how well you perform the techniques of motor skills. Assessing yourself in these areas can provide indicators as to your potential to be skilled in sports and can allow you to monitor your progress in the area of skill development.

There are many different tests that can be used. The tests described below are examples that require few resources and can be easily administered.

A test for coordination

Objective

To assess hand-eye coordination

What is needed for the test

- an administrator
- smooth flat wall
- measuring tape
- chalk or floor tape
- tennis ball
- stopwatch

Setting up the test

- Check that you have a smooth, flat wall and that there are no hazards around the area for the test.

- Use the chalk or the floor tape to mark a line parallel to the wall at a distance of one metre from the wall.

- The administrator controls the time for the test (30 seconds) using a stopwatch, and gives the commands to start and stop. He counts the number of successful catches and records the score.

Instructions to be given by the administrator

- Place both feet behind the one-metre line.

- Hold the tennis ball in one hand (for example, left hand).

- On the command "go", throw the tennis ball against the wall then catch the rebound with your other hand (right hand). Using that hand throw the tennis ball against the wall and catch it again with your other hand (left hand).

- The object of the test is to keep throwing and catching the tennis ball using alternative hands. Your score is the number of successful catches you make in the 30 seconds.

Interpretation of results

The greater the number of catches the better the hand-eye coordination.

A test for balance

Objective

To assess static balance

What is needed for the test

- an administrator

- stopwatch

Setting up the test

- Do the test indoors on a flat floor.

- Check that there are no hazards around the area of the test.

- The person doing the test gets ready by placing hands on hips and placing the toes of one foot against the knee of the other leg.

- The administrator gives the command to start, and uses the stopwatch to time how long the balance is held. This time is recorded.

- The object of the test is to hold the balanced position for as long as possible.

Instructions to be given by the administrator

- Place your hands on your hips and place the toes of one foot against the knee of the other leg.

- On my command of "go", raise your heel off the floor and balance on your toes for as long as you can.

- The test stops if your heel touches the floor, your foot moves away from your knee or your hands come away from your waist.

Interpretation of results

The longer you can hold the position the better your balance.

A test for reaction time
Objective

To assess reaction time

What is needed for the test

- an administrator
- a one-metre ruler

Setting up the test

- The person doing the test places the favoured or dominant lower arm on a desk or small table with the hand beyond the edge of the desk. The index finger and thumb should be outstretched and parallel with the floor.

- The administrator holds the ruler between the person's index finger and thumb so that the top of the thumb is level with the zero centimetre line on the ruler. The administrator releases the ruler at an unknown time to the person doing the test.

- The object of the test is for the person to catch the ruler as soon as possible after it has been released.

- The administrator measures the distance from the zero centimetre line on the ruler to the top of the person's thumb where the ruler was caught.

Instructions to be given by the administrator

- Catch the ruler as soon as possible after it has been released. Hold it in that position.

Interpretation of results

The smaller the measurement in centimetres the faster the reaction time.

A test for agility
Objective

To assess agility

What is needed for the test

- an administrator
- a non-slip surface
- measuring tape
- four cones
- stopwatch

Setting up the test

- Check that you have a non-slip surface and that there are no hazards around the area.

- Place three cones in a straight line with five metres between them. Place the other cone at right angles to these cones, in line with the middle cone and ten metres away from it. This forms a 'T' shape. The test starts at the base of the 'T'.

- The administrator gives the command to start, times the test with a stopwatch, and records the time.

Instructions to be given by the administrator

On my command of "go":

 Run forwards to the middle cone and touch it.

Side step to the left to touch the outer cone.

Side step back to the middle cone to touch it again.

Side step to the right to touch the other outer cone.

Side step back to the middle cone to touch it again.

Run backwards to the cone at the start and touch it.

The test finishes when you touch the last cone.

Interpretation of results

The faster the time the better the agility.

TASK 1 on Skilled performance

Purpose

To analyse the results from assessment tests and seek to draw conclusions from them.

Instructions

Work with a partner and do the coordination, balance, reaction time and agility tests in this section. Record the results.

Bring together the results of as many students as possible and present them in a way that allows comparisons to be made between students.

Can you see any patterns in analysing the results? Can you draw any conclusions?

Improving your coordination, balance, reaction time and agility can aid skilled performance. However, if you want to be skilled in a particular sport such as hockey, basketball, badminton or tennis then you need to learn the skills that are specific to that sport. Understanding the following factors can help you.

Factors to consider when learning skills for sports

Skilled performance or skill is the learnt ability to bring about a predetermined goal/result with maximum certainty and efficiency. What this means is covered in the opening paragraphs of this section.

Learning can be defined as a relatively permanent change in behaviour that occurs as a result of experience and practice, and is not simply due to the process of growing up.

With complex and open skills it can take some time for this state of learning to be achieved, yet along the way there can be progress in learning. This learning demonstrates the relative improvement in performance as a result of guidance and practice undertaken.

The factors that you will consider are:

- the stages of learning
- guidance and learning
- practice and learning
- feedback and learning
- arousal and learning

The stages of learning

Learning can be said to take place in three stages:

- the **cognitive stage**
- the **associative stage**
- the **autonomous stage**

Cognitive stage

The cognitive stage is the first stage and is the beginner stage. It is the thinking stage. You attempt to work out in your mind what you have to do. You have to think hard about how to perform the skill. You have to concentrate and give your full attention to your attempts to perform the sequence of movements. Your movements are not efficient, effective or coordinated, and you make lots of mistakes. You can be anxious, lack confidence, and feel that there is too much to take in. In a competitive situation you can feel lost.

If you persevere, you pass from this stage to the next when you can perform the skill even though it may not be perfectly.

Associative stage

The associative stage is the intermediate, refining stage. You practise the skill over and over again and with feedback you refine your technique (sequence of movements). Gradually you think less and less about the technique and more and more about timing and coordination. You are getting 'into the groove'. Your movements become more efficient, effective and coordinated, and you make fewer and fewer mistakes. You feel more in control and more confident.

In a competitive situation which is reasonably straightforward and without too much pressure, you can use the skill with success. You pass from this stage to the next when you can perform the skill automatically without having to think about your technique or timing.

Autonomous stage

The autonomous stage is the advanced stage. The skill has been learnt, and you are able to perform it automatically without needing to think about it. Your movements are efficient, effective and coordinated, and you make few mistakes. You are in control and confident in yourself. In a competitive situation you are able to take account of relevant factors such as opponents and environmental conditions, adjust yourself accordingly, and successfully perform the skill. You are also able to focus on other important factors of performance such as strategies and tactics and successfully use the skills to implement them.

People learning new skills sometimes get no further than the cognitive stage, and some stay in the associative stage. There is no guarantee that performers reach the autonomous stage. Within the one sport you could have a performer at the cognitive stage for one skill, the associative stage for another skill, and the autonomous stage for another skill.

Guidance and learning

To be able to move successfully through the stages, you need to know and understand the technique of the skill. As outlined earlier, the technique is the sequence of movements carried out to perform the skill efficiently and effectively, and techniques are the building blocks of skilled performance. Sound techniques have to be established in the cognitive stage.

There are three main ways by which guidance on the techniques can be given:

- visual
- verbal (auditory)
- physical/manual

Visual guidance

Visual guidance is when you observe the technique or part of the technique being performed. This can be done through a demonstration, by using a video or DVD clip, or by using photographs.

Verbal guidance

Verbal guidance is when you listen to someone telling you what to do. This should be kept simple and short, especially during the cognitive stage. At all times the language should be clear, concise and consistent in the use of words.

Physical/manual guidance

Physical or manual guidance is when someone physically moves you into position and takes you manually through the sequence of movements.

The most appropriate method depends on the skill. For example, basic skills can usually be learnt quickly from a demonstration. Complex skills need to be broken down into parts and a combination of visual and verbal guidance is usually most successful. Sometimes, even with clear visual and verbal guidance the learner still has difficulty and may need manual guidance.

The most appropriate method also depends on the learner. People usually have a predominant learning style or preferred way of processing information. For example, some people learn best with visual guidance, some with verbal guidance, and some with physical/manual guidance. Some learn best by doing or experiencing – these are **kinaesthetic learners**. Some are **analytic learners** – whether they see, hear or try the skill they need to think about it, retry it, think about it again, and so on.

Practice and learning

You can see the sequence of movements being performed, you can be told how to perform them and you can be physically manipulated through them, but if you don't actually do them yourself and practise them over and over then you won't make progress through the stages of learning. Practice is important. It is practising a skill that develops sound technique and forms a clear and precise memory of the skill.

There are different types of practice:

- whole practice
- part practice
- whole-part-whole practice
- mental practice
- fixed or drill practice
- variable practice
- problem-solving practice
- conditioned games practice

©iStockphoto.com/barsik

Whole practice

Whole practice means practising the skill in its entirety, for example doing the long jump in athletics as you would in a competition – whole practice includes the full sequence of movements for the run-up, takeoff, flight and landing.

Part practice

Part practice means practising one part or section of a skill in isolation. For example, in the long jump you could practise the run-up in isolation. It could be that you have been missing the takeoff board by quite a margin, so you sort out your run and markers and you practise the run-up over and over to ensure you are hitting the takeoff board correctly with your takeoff foot. In some sports like gymnastics and trampolining, certain skills can be too complex or dangerous to be attempted as a whole on your first attempts. Therefore they are built up in parts, where you learn one part of the skill before moving on to the next part and so on.

Whole-part-whole practice

Whole-part-whole practice means practising the skill in its entirety in order to discover any weaknesses in the performance of the skill; if an area of weakness is identified it is corrected and practised in isolation; and the whole skill is then practised again with the identified area of weakness corrected within the performance of the whole skill. For example, in practising the long jump as a whole skill you have noticed that your takeoff is very flat or low to the ground. This weakness is corrected and the corrective actions practised in isolation. You then practise the whole long jump again with the takeoff now being correct within the performance of the whole skill.

Mental practice

Mental practice means visualising yourself doing the skill over and over again in your mind. For example, in the long jump you would visualise yourself setting a personal best jump. The image would include you seeing yourself building up speed on the run-up, driving up powerfully from the takeoff board, running or hanging in the air during flight, and finally stretching out for the landing.

In using mental imagery you should attempt to engage all your senses (seeing, hearing, feeling, touching and smelling) and perform the skill as you would want to in real life. You should see yourself performing the skill very successfully. Your mental image should include details for all aspects of the long jump (run-up, takeoff, flight and landing) and all parts of your body that are involved (leg actions, arm actions, position of the head, etc). The image should also include environmental and other factors (wind, rain, surface, crowd, judges). Once you have the mental image you can focus on any part of it that you want.

Mental practice can be used when you wake up in the morning, before you go to training, during training, after training, or before you go to bed – in other words at any time. All that is required is a few minutes each time you practise it and in total no more than 15 minutes a day.

Fixed or drill practice

Fixed or drill practice means practising the skill under the same conditions each time. This type of practice is most suited to skills from activities such as gymnastics and trampolining where the environment and your opponents don't affect the performance of the skill in a major way. This method could also be used for long jump, or for a skill in a game where you wished the skill or parts of the skill to be repeated over and over with little variation in the playing conditions – for example, standing opposite a partner, 5–10m apart, to practise the chest pass, so no movement about the court is required in performing the practice.

Variable practice

Variable practice means practising the skill in a variety of different contexts and conditions. This type of practice is most suited to net games such as badminton and volleyball, and invasion games such as netball and football, where the contexts and conditions are continually changing. Practice sessions that mirror these changes prepare you so that you can perform the skill in a wide range of situations.

Problem-solving practice

Problem-solving practice means being given situations in which you perform your skills while trying out different solutions. The sports most likely to use this type of practice are net games and invasion games. It involves thinking about strategies and tactics as well as practising your skills.

Conditioned games practice

Conditioned games practice means playing the game but with certain restrictions being applied to it. These restrictions are not normally part of the rules. For example, in hockey or football you could make a condition or restriction that you are only allowed two touches of the ball at any one time. The first touch could be to control the ball, and the second touch must then be a pass or a shot. This conditioned games practice could be used to encourage the skill of passing the ball.

The type and difficulty of the practice you use depends on the complexity of the skill and the stage the learner is at in learning it.

There is a saying, 'Practice makes perfect'. It has since been said, *'Practice makes permanent, but not necessarily perfect'*. This should be a warning about getting the type and quality of practice right.

Timing of practice

The timing of practice can have some affect on learning. Is it better to have one long continuous period of practice to learn new skills or to have the practice spaced out over time? The answer is that there are advantages and disadvantages for each.

Having one continuous block of time allows for continuity in the learning process. However, it can mean that people get tired and bored, and concentration is lost. A continuous block of practice is more effective with learners who have a high level of fitness and are highly motivated.

Having the time split up over a number of weeks allows for short sessions and therefore a shorter time for a focus to be maintained. There is also time for rest and time to practise before the next session. However, if practice is not undertaken between the sessions then what was taught can be lost and little progress made from week to week. Spaced practice is more suited to learners who have lower levels of fitness and experience.

Feedback and learning

Just as good visual and verbal guidance and regular quality practice are vital if the proper techniques of a skill are to be learnt and executed from the start, you also need to receive regular and appropriate feedback. **Feedback** is the information you get on your performance. You need it throughout the stages of learning, but especially in the associative stage.

Intrinsic feedback

Intrinsic (internal) feedback provides information on the 'feel' of performing the sequence of movements. It includes information on balance and on the tension in the muscles. This information comes from the inner ear and from **proprioceptors** in the muscles, tendons and joints. It allows you to make fine adjustments to your movement. Some of the information is responded to without conscious control.

Intrinsic feedback also includes the information gathered from the **interoceptors** in the internal organs of the body, for example the heart, lungs, stomach and intestines. This feedback allows the body systems to respond to the physical demands of the movements involved in the performances.

Extrinsic feedback

Extrinsic (external) feedback provides information on the performance from external sources. This information can be gathered by you, a teacher, a coach, a video clip, or from a movement analysis programme. External information gathered by you is through **exteroceptors**, which are your eyes and ears. Other external feedback is usually presented to you visually or verbally.

There are two categories of extrinsic feedback:

- knowledge of results
- knowledge of performance

Knowledge of results provides basic information on your performance, for example you scored a goal, your service was in, your time was 12 seconds. This can be useful information, but it tells you very little about the quality of the performance.

Knowledge of performance provides information on the quality of your performance. You can get positive feedback on what you did correctly and negative feedback on what you did incorrectly. This feedback allows you to take corrective actions to improve your technique.

Arousal and learning

Arousal is your state of alertness. It is both a physical and mental condition. The physical is controlled by the autonomic nervous system, the role of which is explained later in this section (pages 107–108). The mental is controlled by the brain.

Some people tend naturally to get either over-anxious or over-excited when they have to do things, for example attend an interview, go to a concert, speak to a neighbour, learn new skills, or perform in a competition. This is a **personality trait** of these people and it means that their arousal levels are often very high.

On the other hand, some people tend naturally to be very relaxed and calm about the same things. This is a personality trait of these people and it means that their arousal levels are often very low.

While your personality traits have an influence on your levels of arousal, you may find that it is the specific situation that has a greater influence.

For example, you could get over-anxious or over-excited to the extent that you feel sick when given the opportunity to go caving, whereas another person could be quite relaxed about it. Skydiving may not bother you, but it could make that same other person either over-excited or over-anxious. Similarly, your level of arousal may be fine for playing in an ordinary league match in your sport, but be very high for a cup-final match.

The point is that your personality traits combined with the given situation, influence your level of arousal, and your level of arousal affects how you perform.

There are many theories that try to explain this. Generally, it is agreed that if your arousal level is very low (laid-back, uninterested, unfocused, bored, tired, etc) then you will perform poorly. Likewise, it is agreed that if your arousal level is very high (over-excited, over-anxious, worried, tense, etc) then you will also perform poorly. This means there is an **optimum zone** in between. If your level of arousal is within this zone then you will perform at your best.

Your challenge is get your level of arousal in this optimum zone.

Your level of arousal can be raised through, for example:

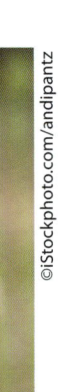

- mental imagery. You can call up images of your goal (to win the league) and vividly remind yourself of what needs to be done to achieve it

- a coach or manager motivating you with a pep talk

- seeing the opposition and their determination

- a coach or manager giving you a special role or job to do

Your level of arousal can be lowered through, for example:

- relaxation techniques. With these, you can lower your heart rate, slow down your breathing and remove tension from your muscles.

- mental imagery. You can imagine yourself performing well and being successful in the competition. This helps take away negative thoughts and worries.

It is a case of getting the balance right for each situation so that optimum arousal is achieved and you can perform at your best.

The complexity of the sport can affect the optimum level of arousal required for peak performance. The greater the complexity of the sport the lower the level of arousal needed. For example, golf is more complex than weightlifting and requires finer motor skills, so it requires a lower level of arousal for peak performances; weightlifting is less complex a sport and requires gross motor skills, so it requires a higher level of arousal for peak performance.

Information processing and the nervous system

The nervous system gathers information from inside and outside the body and sends it to the **central nervous system (CNS)**. This information is processed and interpreted in the brain, and a decision is made on what to do. The information on the response is then sent to the appropriate parts of the body so they carry out the response.

Main parts

The nervous system consists of two parts:

- the **central nervous system (CNS)**
- the **peripheral nervous system (PNS)**

The central nervous system (CNS) consists of the brain and spinal cord. The spinal cord carries information from the body to the brain. The brain interprets the information and makes a decision. The information on the response is passed from the brain through the spinal cord to the rest of the body.

The peripheral nervous system (PNS) consists of the nerves going from the CNS to all parts of the body. There are two types of nerves in the PNS:

- **sensory nerves**
- **motor nerves**

Sensory nerves take information from the **receptors** (**exteroceptors**, **proprioceptors** and **interoceptors**) to the CNS. The receptors sense changes in the internal or external environments.

Motor nerves take information from CNS to the **effectors**. The effectors carry out the response of the CNS, and are usually the muscles.

The PNS has two parts:

- the **somatic nervous system**
- the **autonomic nervous system**

The somatic nervous system deals with information from the external environment (light, sound, pressure, etc).

The autonomic nervous system deals with information from the internal environment (internal organs like the heart, lungs, stomach, intestines, etc).

The autonomic nervous system has two sub-systems:

- the **sympathetic nervous system**
- the **parasympathetic nervous system**

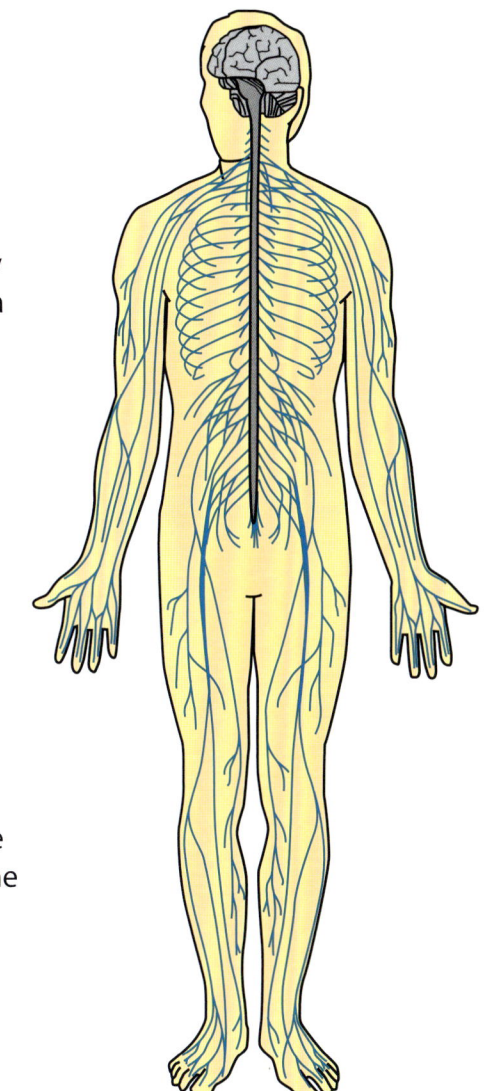

The sympathetic nervous system prepares the body for 'fight or flight'. It gets the body prepared for action.

The parasympathetic nervous system does the opposite of the sympathetic system by calming and relaxing the body.

The nervous systems in action

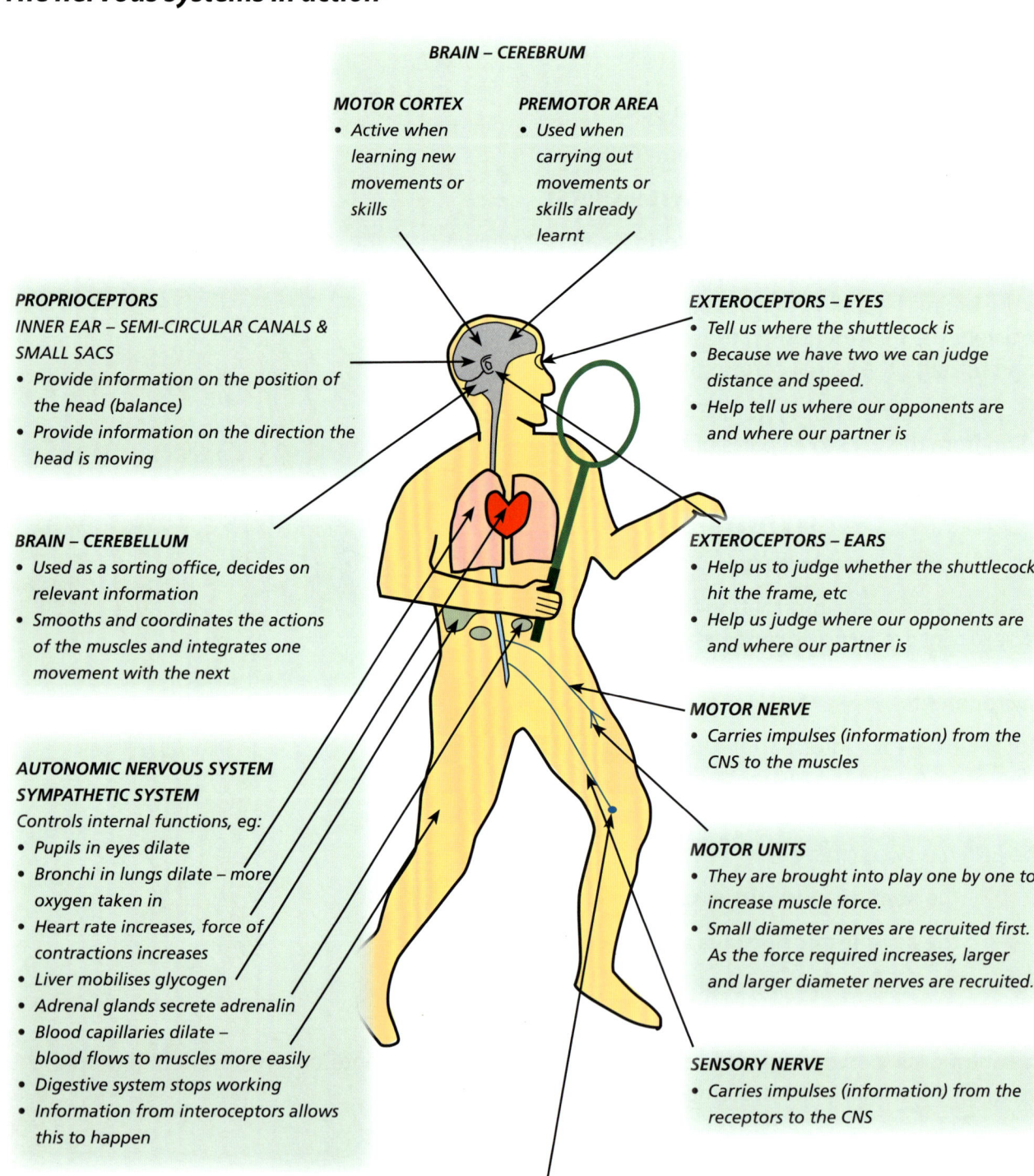

BRAIN – CEREBRUM

MOTOR CORTEX
- *Active when learning new movements or skills*

PREMOTOR AREA
- *Used when carrying out movements or skills already learnt*

PROPRIOCEPTORS
INNER EAR – SEMI-CIRCULAR CANALS & SMALL SACS
- *Provide information on the position of the head (balance)*
- *Provide information on the direction the head is moving*

EXTEROCEPTORS – EYES
- *Tell us where the shuttlecock is*
- *Because we have two we can judge distance and speed.*
- *Help tell us where our opponents are and where our partner is*

BRAIN – CEREBELLUM
- *Used as a sorting office, decides on relevant information*
- *Smooths and coordinates the actions of the muscles and integrates one movement with the next*

EXTEROCEPTORS – EARS
- *Help us to judge whether the shuttlecock hit the frame, etc*
- *Help us judge where our opponents are and where our partner is*

MOTOR NERVE
- *Carries impulses (information) from the CNS to the muscles*

AUTONOMIC NERVOUS SYSTEM
SYMPATHETIC SYSTEM
Controls internal functions, eg:
- *Pupils in eyes dilate*
- *Bronchi in lungs dilate – more oxygen taken in*
- *Heart rate increases, force of contractions increases*
- *Liver mobilises glycogen*
- *Adrenal glands secrete adrenalin*
- *Blood capillaries dilate – blood flows to muscles more easily*
- *Digestive system stops working*
- *Information from interoceptors allows this to happen*

MOTOR UNITS
- *They are brought into play one by one to increase muscle force.*
- *Small diameter nerves are recruited first. As the force required increases, larger and larger diameter nerves are recruited.*

SENSORY NERVE
- *Carries impulses (information) from the receptors to the CNS*

PROPRIOCEPTORS – MUSCLES, TENDONS, JOINTS
- *Provide information on muscle tension, how stretched the muscles are, and on the angle of the joints*

Information-processing in the brain

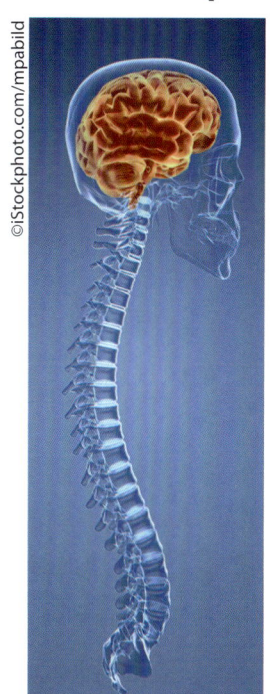

©iStockphoto.com/mpabild

In learning a skill the eyes see the demonstration and the ears hear the instructions.

What your eyes observed and what your ears heard is transformed into neural information and transmitted to the brain. This is known as the **input**.

Within a **sensory register** in the brain, **selective perception** takes place. In other words you select the information that you think is important, while all other information is discarded or forgotten. This happens in milliseconds, and is known as **short-term sensory storage (STSS)**.

The selected information is then temporarily stored as working memory or **short-term memory (STM)**. Only a limited amount of information can be held as working memory and only for up to 20 seconds without it being repeated. During this time, **long-term memory (LTM)** is activated to make sense of the information. Previously-learnt experiences are compared with the new information to determine whether it is worth permanently retaining it for future recall. If it is, the information is encoded and stored as LTM. The critical thing is getting the information to be meaningfully encoded and placed in the LTM in an organised manner. The more connections that the LTM is able to make with the information, the less processing power is needed to encode the information, making it more likely that you will have learnt the skill. With fewer connections, more processing power is needed to encode the information, so you are further away from learning the skill. The brain's LTM has a limitless capacity and is therefore able to store all motor skills that can be learnt.

A **response generator** handles the way you organise your response to the information. This is known as the **output**. The response is transmitted to the muscles (the effectors) and you make your attempt to perform the sequence of movements of the skill.

Feedback on the performance helps learning.

 ## TASK 2 on Skilled performance

Purpose

To apply concepts and principles to a specific situation.

Instructions

- Choose a sport and a basic skill that you have learnt in that sport.

- Taking into consideration how we learn skills, write down the verbal instructions that you would give to explain the proper technique for performing the skill.

Remember, verbal guidance should be kept simple and short. The language should be clear, concise and consistent in the use of words.

TASK 3 on Skilled performance

Purpose

To apply concepts and principles to a specific situation.

Instructions

- Choose a sport and a basic skill that you have learnt in that sport.
- Taking into consideration what mental imagery is and what mental practice is, describe in detail your performance of that skill in a situation.

Remember, mental imagery should include details of all aspects of the performance.

 SUMMARY

In this section the focus changed from developing physical wellbeing and fitness to developing skilled performances.

There are lots of different ways that sports skills can be classified but one thing that they all have in common is that skills are learnt.

Coordination, balance, reaction time and agility are linked with the performance of skills, but to be a skilled performer in a particular sport you need to learn the skills that are specific to that sport.

Learning specific sports skills can be a long process. It can help if you understand how the nervous system controls movement and how information is processed by the brain.

It will also help if you understand that you go through three stages in learning skills and

©iStockphoto.com/dennysb

that the guidance that you are given, for example visual or verbal, can make all the difference to the quality of your learning.

Once you have the proper technique established in your head, practice, practice and more practice combined with quality feedback on your performances is needed for the technique to become a learnt skill. There are many different types of practice that can help you do this.

Finally, how well you progress will depend on your personality and your levels of concentration, confidence, control and commitment.

Section 11
Other factors

©iStockphoto.com/ericsphotography

Other factors that affect participation and performance in physical activity

In Section 1 you considered the concepts of health, physical fitness and skill. In Section 2 you studied how a range of factors from your lifestyle like diet, smoking and exercise affect your physical wellbeing. In Sections 3 to 7 you focused on exercise and training. In these sections you studied what type of exercise you should do to maintain good physical health or to be physically fit for physical activities or sport, what training methods to use, what principles to follow to ensure the exercise/training is effective, how to assess progress, and finally the effects that the exercise/training has on your body systems to make you fitter. In Section 8 you looked at factors that can influence your overall potential to perform in physical activities or sports and in Section 9 you looked at health and safety issues with participation. In Section 10 the focus was on skill development for physical activities or sport.

In this section you will look at a range of factors that may account for people getting involved in, and then becoming and remaining committed participants in, physical activities or sport.

For each of the factors you will want to consider its influence:

- in getting people involved in the first place
- in keeping them as committed participants
- on performances

Personality traits/characteristics and the nature of physical activities

©iStockphoto.com/aabejon

Personality traits/characteristics describe the way you are and what distinguishes you from others.

For example, some people are shy, sensitive, inward-looking, careful, like to do things alone and are often not confident in themselves. These people are known as **introverts**. Others are outgoing, mix well with people, optimistic and are confident about themselves. They are known as **extroverts**.

The nature of physical activities also differs. For example, some are team activities while others are individual activities; some involve physical contact while others don't; some involve using equipment while others don't; and some are played indoors while others are played outdoors.

Bring the personality traits/characteristics together with the nature of the physical activities and you find that certain types of people prefer some physical activities over others. Introverts tend to prefer activities which don't involve physical contact, and so generally participate and perform better in individual activities rather than team games – for example, archery, diving, golf and sailing. Extroverts on the other hand seek thrills and thrive on competition. They tend to participate and perform better in team activities which involve physical contact, such as football, rugby, ice hockey and judo.

The better the match between a person's personality traits/characteristics and the nature of physical activities, the more likely they are to perform better and become committed participants.

Enjoyment

Enjoyment is the act of receiving pleasure from something.

If you have a good time participating in a physical activity, you will probably want to repeat the experience. If this continues to be the case then you are likely to become a committed participant. If you enjoy an activity then you often want to improve your performance in it. This is not always the case, however – many people are not particularly good at their physical activities and their performances don't improve much, yet they enjoy participating at their own level and so they continue to be involved.

©iStockphoto.com/barsik

If you do not enjoy participating in an activity then you are more likely to give it up.

Socialising

©iStockphoto.com/bonniej

Socialising is about mixing with others and being comfortable with them.

Team sports provide the framework for people to work with and comply with others, and to compete against other teams. Often you begin participating in an activity or sport through someone asking you to. The sport is the initial bond and if you feel comfortable with the people involved and the expectations they have of you, friendships tend to form within teams. Socialising can extend beyond the normal sports setting, for example going out for a meal or visiting each other's homes.

Being part of a team and not wanting to let others down can keep you committed, encourage you to work hard in training, and inspire you to perform to the best of your ability for the team.

On the other hand, some people have no desire to be part of a team and find the social aspect uncomfortable. As a result, they are not likely to become committed participants in team games.

Release

Release means being freed from an obligation or duty.

Participating in physical activities or sport can allow people to take their minds off obligations and duties. Having experienced the benefits they then want to continue participating.

It could be that studying for your GCSEs each day needs great concentration and the opportunity to take part in physical activity provides a release or freedom from that tension. For example, after a hard day's work in school you could find that going for a run, going dancing or playing hockey provides a release that allows the tension to disappear and the rebuilding of energy to take place.

On the other hand, some people may find school repetitive, boring, and tedious and the opportunity to go skydiving or rock climbing at the weekends can provide a release for them.

The release that is experienced can make people committed participants. It is this experience that is most important and not so much the actual performance.

Competition

Competition is when you engage in a contest. It could be against one or more entrants, a set standard, or nature and the elements.

Many people are competitive by nature. They want to challenge themselves against others or against standards. Physical activities and sports provide opportunities for competition, for example knockout or league-type competitions.

Knockout competitions allow you to compete against a wide range of abilities. However, once you are beaten you are out of the competition. With league-type competitions you play everyone in your group, and the groups are usually arranged so that people are competing against others of a similar standard.

Competitions provide opportunities for enjoyment, excitement, success, and socialising. Entering a competition is a way of getting people involved in a physical activity or sport. Competitions are a major factor in keeping many people committed participants. People who are successful want to continue to show that they are the best and to maintain their performances at a high level. People who do not do well want to prove that they can do better and they will work to improve their performances. This instinct keeps them committed participants who want to perform to the best of their ability.

Some, however, find competitions off-putting. They are unlikely to participate unless they can do so at a purely recreational level.

Excitement

Excitement is when your feelings are aroused in pleasurable anticipation of something.

The opportunity to try a new activity or sport can be exciting. This pleasurable anticipation encourages you to actually try out the activity in the first place. If you feel excited about trying it again then you are likely to do so. If this excitement continues because you want to mix with friends who do the activity, because you are good at it, because you like the competition it offers, or for other reasons, then you are more likely to become a committed participant.

On the other hand, if you are not at all excited by the opportunity to play a particular sport, then you probably won't bother. Similarly, if you try a sport and find it boring or you dread going back, even if you had at first been excited about trying it, then you are unlikely to become a committed participant. This zone can depend on your personality and the type of sport.

Excitement can also affect your performances. Both overexcitement and lack of excitement can make your performance suffer. There is an optimum zone of arousal for you to perform at your best. See Section 10, pages 105–106, for more details.

Success

Success is when an outcome has been favourably achieved.

The outcome can vary from person to person. For some it could be to enjoy themselves, while for others it could be to win competitions.

Whatever your outcomes, if you consistently succeed in achieving them then you are more likely to become a committed participant in whatever sport you do. It is said that success breeds success.

Sport provides opportunities for you to be able to cope with success and failure.

In competitive sport there are always winners and losers. Winning can inspire you to improve your performances even further, and losing can make you analyse what went wrong and work to improve your performances for the future.

©iStockphoto.com/mr_wilke

Encouragement

©iStockphoto.com/nano

Encouragement is inspiring someone with the courage or confidence to do something. It can also involve helping or supporting them.

It can sometimes be daunting to get involved in a new sport or to enter a competition; it can be difficult to master a skill; it can be disappointing when performances are below standard; and it can be frustrating when you are not winning. It is in situations such as these that encouragement can keep you going and keep you involved.

Encouragement could be simply a few words said to you by your parents, your coach or a team-mate, but these words give you confidence. It could be your coach trying a different way to help you to learn a skill, or your parents transporting you to competitions and staying to watch you perform.

With encouragement you are more likely to become a committed participant and want to perform your best. Being continually criticised or put down can have the opposite effect.

Motivation (extrinsic and intrinsic)

Motivation is the desire or drive you have to do something.

The greater your desire or drive, the more likely that you will become a committed participant. If you have little desire or drive then you are more likely to drop out. Your desire could be due to the excitement you get from participating, the thrill of competing, or the comradeship of being part of a team.

©iStockphoto.com/barsik

Your motivation can be **extrinsic** or **intrinsic**.

Extrinsic motivation is when you are motivated by things *outside* you, for example the desire to win medals, cups, money, or even to please other people.

Intrinsic motivation is when the desire comes from *inside* you – you are participating because you love to compete, win or lose. People participating with intrinsic motivation are more likely to become and stay committed participants. Like those who are extrinsically motivated, they can have external goals such as winning a cup or a medal, but if they fail to achieve their goal they do not lose their motivation.

Setting goals can help with motivation. They give you something to aim for, make your training purposeful, and allow you to set your own success criteria. The greater your motivation or desire, the more likely you will want to do your best and be willing to work hard to improve your performances.

⬤ Career opportunities

Stu Forster/Getty Images

Career opportunities are the openings available to earn a living from sport.

Many young people dream of being successful professional sportspeople. It is this that gets them interested in the first place, and keeps them participating in the hope that they will be discovered or that their performances will merit monetary recognition. The dream can inspire them to continually work at improving their performances.

Unfortunately for most, it is only the best who are able to achieve this and, from their participation, gain sufficient money to earn a livelihood. The very best can earn huge amounts of money, the best a livelihood, some can survive on their earnings combined with other part-time employment, but for most there is very little chance of having a career based on their participation and performances in a sport.

Although there are very few who make it as professional athletes or players, there are other career opportunities associated with sport that those who are committed may enter. For example, it is possible for some to find a career in coaching, management or marketing; or as a referee, groundsman or fitness consultant.

⬤ Cultural heritage

Cultural heritage is the passing on and reinforcing of shared traditions from one generation to the next. These traditions can be national, local or family-based.

If your parents play a sport, there is a good chance that you will be influenced by this. If your parents play tennis they might have taken you to the tennis courts from a young age. At first, you would have retrieved the tennis balls, but would soon have been given a mini racket and your parents would have played with you. Soon you would have been taught to play, and perhaps received coaching. You might then have become involved in junior competitions, and your parents are likely to have supported you when you were playing. In no time playing tennis would have become a habit for you.

When you become an adult with your own children, you will probably also take them to the tennis courts. They will go through similar experiences to you when you were young. These experiences will be reinforced by your children's grandparents. This all leads to playing tennis becoming a tradition in the family.

The process can be similar in the local community or at national level. For example, some schools have developed a tradition of playing rugby, others a tradition of playing football, and others a tradition of playing Gaelic games. If you go to a school that has a particular tradition then there is a good chance that you will become part of that tradition. Local communities can set up clubs that become successful, and this success attracts young members. If this continues then the next generation will also be attracted. and it soon becomes a community that has a tradition in that particular sport. If lots of local communities have clubs that develop similar traditions in a sport, then the sport can become a *national* tradition.

It is possible for countries to have more than one national sport. For example, rugby and cricket are associated with being traditional national sports in Australia, skiing with being a national sport in Austria, and basketball and baseball with being two traditional national sports in the USA.

When sports become traditions for families, local communities or countries, a lot of expectation can be put on participants' performances.

Peer pressure

Peer pressure is the influence that people of similar social standing and age can have on each other.

We like to be part of a social group. Within a group there will be those who exert more influence than others.

With regard to participation and performance in sport, this influence can be positive or negative. For example, if your peers enjoy being involved in a particular sport then it is likely that you will stick with the group and become involved in it as well.

If, on the other hand, the group is against participating in physical activities or sport, then the chances are that you will not participate either. You may have an interest in a sport but because of comments or jibes by your peers you will feel pressurised to conform with them.

Peer pressure can also have a positive or negative effect on performance. For some, knowing the expectations of their peers can lift them and they perform well. For others, high expectations from their peers can make them fall apart and they perform poorly.

Affluence

Affluence is when there is an abundant supply of money available to spend, after having paid for all essential outgoings.

Someone who is affluent is rich or wealthy. Being wealthy means that there are opportunities to participate in physical activities or sports that are expensive. For example, you could buy your own yacht for sailing, have your own horse for equestrian events, be involved in motor-sport racing with your own car or bike, or be able to go to skiing in the USA or Europe for a month each year. It can mean being able to afford being a member of a golf club or an exclusive gym.

If you have very little money to spare after paying for all essential outgoings, then you will be limited in what physical activities or sports you will be able to do. For example, you could be limited to walking or running from your home, swimming, or attending the gym at your local leisure centre.

Being affluent or wealthy does mean that you can sample a wider range of activities compared to someone who isn't, but it doesn't necessarily mean that you will become more of a committed participant in your activities.

Affluence can have an influence on performance in that a wealthy person can, for example, afford to employ a personal trainer or pay for golf lessons or extra coaching to help them improve. The same opportunities would not be available to a less wealthy person.

Education

Education is the process of acquiring knowledge and skills through formal instruction during childhood and adolescence.

There are 12 years of compulsory education for all children and young people. What they experience of physical activities and sport in those 12 years can influence them for life. If they experience quality physical education and sport during that time, then there is a good chance that they will become involved in physical activity and sport inside and outside of school, and that they will continue as committed participants when they leave school. If their experiences are bad or limited then there is less chance of them participating when they leave school.

The 12 years of education can also affect their performances in physical activities and sport. Physical Education and school sport help young people learn how to improve their performances in a wide range of activities.

Occupation

Occupation is what job or profession a person has.

If your job or profession is well paid then it allows opportunities to take part in activities that may be expensive. If, however, you are unemployed you will be limited as to what you can do because of financial restraints. The points made opposite under affluence apply here.

If you work from nine to five and are off at the weekends then you would be available for team training and for matches. However, not everyone works these hours. For example, some doctors have to work longer hours and weekends, as do some businessmen and women. Some people work shifts where, for a time, they may work from seven in the morning to three in the afternoon. They then work a shift from three in the afternoon to eleven at night; and finally a shift from eleven at night to seven in the morning.

People who have long hours or who work shifts can find it difficult to make a commitment to competitive team sports. They are often not available for training and for matches at the weekends. These work patterns can also affect their performances.

Some people find their jobs repetitive or tedious and therefore outside the job they want to participate in sport they find exciting and thrilling. Some people find their jobs hectic and busy, so they favour an activity or sport that provides a release from this.

Leisure time

Leisure time is free time. It is the time available for you to choose what you want to do, and excludes time at work or school, the time needed for other chores or commitments, and the time needed for essential maintenance like sleeping, washing and eating.

If your occupation allows a lot of leisure time then you have the freedom to be involved in whatever activities you wish. However, if you don't have much time, or if your leisure time is at unusual times because of shift work, you will be limited in your choice of activity or sport.

If you are unemployed then you will have lots of free time, but will be limited as what to you can do because of financial restraints.

The amount of leisure time you have and when you have it can affect your performance. Having lots of free time means you can practise to improve your performance.

Age

©iStockphoto.com/Paha_L

In many sports, your **age** controls what events or competitions you will be allowed to participate in. For example, you are not allowed to enter a marathon when you are young. In other sports you will be required to compete with others in your age group. This is to keep children safe and have them compete against other children at a similar stage of development.

Age categories can also be applied to the elderly. In some competitions there are categories for older age groups such as the over-fifties.

Your age can also affect your performances. When you are young you have not fully developed your motor and physical capabilities and so you can't perform as well as when you become a mature adult. As you get older your physical capabilities start to deteriorate and you can't perform as well when you were a mature adult. See Section 8, page 84, for more information on this.

Geographical location

Geographical location refers to the natural features of a place.

These can influence what sports and physical activities can be done in the area. For example, if you live near the sea or a lake where water sports consistently take place, then there is a good chance that you will get involved. If, however, you live more than 50 miles from the sea or lake then you are less likely to get involved in a water sport and become a committed participant. Likewise, if you live in a high mountainous area that has lots of snow each winter, then there is more chance of you participating in a sport such as skiing than if you live in an area like Northern Ireland.

Climate

Climate is the long-term customary weather conditions of an area.

Northern Ireland's geographical position means that it is never too hot in the summer or too cold in the winter, and we get lots of rainfall throughout the year. Our unreliable weather can discourage people from participating in activities such as tennis and cricket.

For those who do participate, performance can be affected as practice time can be limited or broken up because of the weather.

Facilities

Facilities are the buildings or amenities that allow organised sport and physical activities to take place, for example swimming pools, indoor basketball courts, tennis courts, pitches for team games, and golf courses.

The existence of facilities in an area can affect participation. For example, if an area has a swimming pool there will probably be a swimming club. The pool will also be used by recreational swimmers and people who take part in other water-based activities. Having easy access to the facility means that anyone with an interest in swimming will use the pool. However, if there is no swimming pool nearby people will be reluctant to travel great distances in order to have a swim.

Facilities can affect performance. If there are no facilities available in the local area so people have to travel, they become tired from the travelling and training, and this affects their performances. Outdated and poorly-maintained facilities can also have a negative impact on performance.

Technology

Technology is the application of practical or mechanical sciences to sport. It is often seen through improvements being made to facilities or equipment.

Technological advances can attract new people into sports. For example, hockey is mostly played now on artificial turf rather than grass or quarry-dust pitches.

However, because the technological advances are usually associated with *improving* performances this factor is more influential in sustaining the interest of those who are already participating. For example, tennis rackets and golf clubs are continually being improved so that those using them can get more power and be more accurate.

Government (central, local and sports bodies)

Central

Central government affects participation and performance in sport because:

- They decide on the country's overall policy for sport.
- They pass laws/orders that provide the legal framework for the implementation of the policy.

- They are responsible for setting up bodies like the Sports Council, to look after the implementation and regulation of the policy and orders for sport.

- They provide subsidies or grants to organisations for sports provision.

- They decide the place of physical education and sport in the school curriculum.

You may question why there are no facilities in your area, why you cannot get coaching to help you to improve your performance, or why there is so little time spent on physical education in school. The reasons can often lead back to government policy.

Local

Local councils are set up by Acts of Parliament. Councils' responsibilities are determined and controlled by central government. Councils in Northern Ireland affect participation and performance in sport and physical recreation because they have a statutory responsibility for the provision of leisure services, and therefore are the main providers of physical recreation and sport.

Councils provide facilities such as leisure centres, swimming pools, playing fields, tennis courts, bowling greens, and amenities such as parks and gardens.

Councils develop leisure services because:

- leisure services improve the quality of life for local people.

- new services and facilities create employment and assist the local economy.

- improved amenities and new attractions help to encourage tourism and attract business.

- improved quality of life helps to attract businesses to the area. An attractive environment with good amenities is a factor in the choice of sites for factories and homes for business executives.

Councils are mainly funded through central government grants and local taxation in the form of rates. They also receive money from charges made for the use of facilities.

Sports bodies

Governing bodies of sport affect participation and performance because:

- they determine the rules and laws of the sport.

- they organise competitions within their country and internationals against other countries.

- they organise the education of coaches.

- they organise coaching courses for performers.

- They are responsible for the running of the sport and the conduct of all those involved in it. They provide guidelines on what is considered to be ethical or unethical behaviour in their sport, ensure that all decisions are made in accordance with their code of ethics, and see that sanctions are consistently applied.

Sports clubs are affiliated to their particular governing body.

Media

©iStockphoto.com/realPHOTO

The **media** or mass media refers to the means of communication that reach large numbers of people in a short time, such as the internet, television, radio, newspapers and magazines.

The media can influence participation and performance because they decide what sports to cover and to what depth. Some sports can be overexposed while others receive very little coverage. The media are concerned about viewing figures and ratings and the number of hits or copies sold, so they will cover what they think people will be most interested in.

Their coverage can reinforce cultural traditions, or alternatively can open up communities to new sports.

Some argue that the coverage of sport inspires people to participate. On the other hand, others argue that the coverage turns people into 'couch spectators' who are more interested in watching sport in the comfort of their homes than actually participating in it.

The media generally gives considerable coverage to sport, so the top sportspeople become well-known and the public wants to find out more and more about them. The media can then go beyond reporting on and criticising their performances in sport and report on and criticise their private lives. This aspect can affect the performances of some of these sportspeople.

TASK on Other factors

Purpose

To research examples that illustrate how a factor may get people involved in a sport, keep them as committed participants, or affect their performance.

Instructions

Choose five factors and for each describe an example that illustrates how the factor can affect participation.

Choose five factors and for each describe an example that illustrates how the factor can affect performance.

SUMMARY

In this section you have covered many factors that can in some way affect participation or performance in sport. In reality it is usually a combination of these factors that accounts for your participation or non-participation in a sport and the actual level of your performances.

Section 12

Exercise/training session

In this section you will learn what steps to follow to plan safe, appropriate and effective exercise sessions for developing the components of physical fitness (see Section 3).

The best way to learn this is to practise following the steps and to get the feel for effectively applying the methods and principles of training covered in Sections 4 and 5.

To check your understanding, you should get other students to evaluate your attempts at planning. In return, you should evaluate their attempts. In this way you will help each other to learn these skills.

You will also be responsible for building up a bank of safe and appropriate exercises that you will be able to use in your exercise/training sessions.

Planning a safe, appropriate and effective exercise/training session

An exercise/training session is the time you spend on exercising or training at one go.

An exercise/training session normally includes:

- a warm-up
- a workout
- a cool-down

This applies to health-related exercise sessions and to training sessions to develop peak physical fitness.

124

⭕ Planning a safe, appropriate and effective warm-up ━━━━

Why have a warm-up?

The purpose of the warm-up is to:

- 🟢 prepare your body systems for the workout
- 🟢 minimise the risk of muscle and joint injury
- 🟢 prepare yourself mentally for the workout

A safe, appropriate and effective warm-up should include:

- 🟢 **pulse-raising activity**
- 🟢 **mobility exercises**
- 🟢 **flexibility exercises**

The reason for including pulse-raising activity in the warm-up is:

- 🟢 to gradually and moderately work the heart and lungs in preparation for the workout
- 🟢 to redirect blood from some internal organs to the muscles
- 🟢 to increase the blood flow to the muscles
- 🟢 to raise body temperature. Warm muscles are less likely to tear.

Pulse-raising activity involves working the major muscles of the body in rhythmic movements, for example jogging. You could use a variety of other activities, like cycling or rowing.

The reason for including mobility exercises in the warm-up is to loosen up the joints so that they move more freely. This involves gently and rhythmically moving the bones at the joints so that the synovial fluid is warmed and becomes less viscous (less thick and gooey). There are also lots of different mobility exercises you could choose from to provide variety.

The reason for including flexibility exercises in the warm-up is to stretch the muscles, tendons and ligaments at the joints so that there is less chance of muscle or joint injury. This involves doing a range of static flexibility exercises. Again, there are lots of different flexibility exercises to choose from to provide variety.

Generally the harder your workout is going to be, the longer you should spend warming up.

An outline of a warm-up

A typical warm-up before undertaking a strenuous workout would be jogging for a time until you start to sweat, then alternating periods of jogging with mobility exercises for the neck, shoulders, arms, spine, hips, knees and ankles.

When you are warmed up and loose from this you would do static flexibility exercises for the muscles of the neck, shoulders, arms, trunk, hips, and legs.

You may then increase the pulse-raising activity from jogging to running so that the intensity is closer to the demands of the workout.

Planning the pulse-raising activities

1. Choose a safe and appropriate pulse-raising activity.

The pulse-raising activity should match the type of exercise that you are going to use in the workout. This is applying the principle of specificity (see Section 5, pages 54–55). You should be able to describe the type of exercise to be done.

2. Decide on the intensity.

You should start with low-intensity work and gradually raise the intensity towards the level to be used in the workout. This is applying the principle of overload (see Section 5, pages 55–57).

3. Decide on the time.

The time will depend on the individual and the outside temperature. Generally when your body starts to sweat it means that you have warmed up. This is applying the principle of overload.

©iStockphoto.com/markp73

An example to illustrate this:

1. *Choose a safe and appropriate pulse-raising activity*.

If you are going to run in your workout you should use jogging as your pulse-raising activity in your warm-up, as this matches what you are going to do in the workout.

2. *Decide on the intensity*.

Start with a slow jog and gradually increase the pace of the jog.

3. *Decide on the time*.

The time will depend on the individual and the outside temperature. It could be between seven to ten minutes. When your body starts to sweat it means that you have warmed up and you can introduce mobility exercises.

Planning the mobility exercises

1. Choose safe and appropriate mobility exercises.

The mobility exercises should cover the major joints (neck, shoulders, arms, spine, hips, knees and ankles), or as a minimum the joints used in the workout. This is applying the principle of specificity. You should be able to describe and illustrate how the mobility exercises should be performed.

2. Decide on the intensity.

The bones at the joints should be moved gently and rhythmically within their normal range of movement. This is applying the principle of overload.

3. Decide on the time.

The time will depend on the individual and the outside temperature. Do the mobility exercises until the joints are moving freely, for example 30 seconds for each exercise. This is applying the principle of overload.

An example to illustrate this:

1. *Choose safe and appropriate mobility exercises*.

To mobilise or loosen up your shoulder joints you could hold up your arms at shoulder height with your elbows bent and your hands near your chin. You would then make circles with both elbows, first going in a backwards direction and then in a forwards direction.

2. *Decide on the intensity*.

The elbows should be moved gently and rhythmically in small circles, within the normal range of movement allowed at the shoulder joints.

3. *Decide on the time*.

The elbows should be circled forwards for 20 seconds and then backwards for 20 seconds, or until the shoulder joints feel loosened and are moving freely.

This is a safe mobility exercise as it gently and rhythmically works the shoulder joints within their normal range of movement. It is also appropriate, as it allows the shoulder joints to warm up and move more freely.

Planning the flexibility exercises

1. Choose safe and appropriate flexibility exercises.

The selected exercises should cover the major muscles of the body (neck, shoulders, arms, chest, trunk, hips and legs), or as a minimum the muscles that will be used in the workout. Static flexibility exercises should be used (see Section 4, page 52). This is applying the principle of specificity. You should be able to describe and illustrate how the flexibility exercises should be performed.

©iStockphoto.com/leezsnow

2. Decide on the intensity.

The muscle should be slowly stretched to its limit, then stretched a little further until mild tension is felt. This is applying the principle of overload.

3. Decide on the time.

The muscle should be held in the stretched position under mild tension for between 5 and 15 seconds in a warm-up. This is applying the principle of overload.

An example to illustrate this:

1. *Choose safe and appropriate flexibility exercises*.

To stretch the hamstrings (muscles at rear of your upper leg) you could lie on your back on the floor. With one leg remaining flat on the floor you lift the other leg up towards your chest. You then take hold of this leg with both hands. Keeping the leg reasonably straight, gently pull it towards your chest.

2. Decide on the intensity.

Hold the upright leg with both hands and gently pull it towards your chest until mild tension is felt in the hamstring muscles.

3. Decide on the time.

The leg should be held in the stretched position under mild tension for ten seconds.

This exercise is safe because your body weight is supported on the floor and it is appropriate as it will stretch the hamstring muscles of the leg. The time is sufficient as it is within the range of 5 to 15 seconds.

Evaluating the safety, appropriateness and effectiveness of a warm-up

1. Judge whether the warm-up includes *pulse-raising activity*, *mobility exercises* and *flexibility exercises*. If any of the three are missing you should point this out and explain why they should be included in the warm-up.

2. Judge whether the *pulse-raising activity* is safe and appropriate for the workout, and whether the *intensity* and *time* provide a suitable overload for the warm-up. If you see a problem you should say what is wrong and be able to explain an appropriate alternative.

3. Judge whether the *mobility exercises* are safe and appropriate for the workout, and whether the *intensity* and *time* provide a suitable overload for the warm-up. If you see a problem you should say what is wrong and be able to explain an appropriate alternative.

4. Judge whether the *flexibility exercises* are safe and appropriate for the workout, and whether the *intensity* and *time* provide a suitable overload for the warm-up. If you see a problem you should say what is wrong and be able to explain an appropriate alternative.

▷ TASK 1 on Exercise/training session

Purpose

To build up a bank of safe and appropriate mobility exercises suitable for warm-ups, and to be able to describe and illustrate how they should be performed to make them effective.

Instructions

Research and select safe and appropriate mobility exercises for each of the following joints – neck, shoulders, arms, spine, hips, knees and ankles.

Describe and illustrate, with the use of stick diagrams, how the mobility exercises should be performed to make them effective.

Planning a safe, appropriate and effective workout

The workout is the conditioning phase when the work is done to develop one or more of the seven components of physical fitness – aerobic and anaerobic; muscular power, strength, speed and endurance; and flexibility.

Planning to develop the aerobic or anaerobic energy systems

First consider the goal and what is expected (health-related or performance-related). Consider the gender, age, weight, body type, present level of fitness and personal preferences of the individual.

The goal and the information available on the individual should be kept in mind when making the following decisions.

1. Choose a safe and appropriate type of exercise and training method.

Type of exercise

©iStockphoto.com/dsabo

You should choose the type of exercise that best matches what you intend to achieve through the workout. If you are exercising to maintain good health then you can choose from a variety of activities such as running, swimming, dancing, cycling or rowing. Any of these activities can be used to develop aerobic energy production.

However, if you are training for something more specific, such as a 10km road race, then the type of exercise must be specific to the event – in this case running.

Training method (See Section 4.)

For the development of aerobic fitness you could choose from continuous steady-pace, fartlek, interval or circuit training. These training methods can be applied to the different types of exercise, for example swimming, running or cycling. When the goal is for health, continuous steady-pace training is the method most frequently used.

When the goal is more specific and demanding, the other training methods will be used as well. When the goal is to develop anaerobic fitness, interval training is the method most frequently used. This is applying the principle of specificity.

2. Decide an appropriate intensity.

The intensity will be determined by whether you want to develop aerobic or anaerobic fitness. For both you need to know the minimum intensity needed for a benefit to be gained (the threshold), and you need to know if there is an upper limit over which you should not go.

Remember, in deciding the intensity you must take into account what exercise the person is already doing and their level of fitness in that component, so that you can overload appropriately. This is one way of applying the principle of overload.

The table on pages 43–45 shows the differences between developing aerobic and anaerobic fitness through using interval training.

3. Decide an appropriate time/number of repetitions and sets.

For both the aerobic and anaerobic components you need to know the minimum time (or number of repetitions and sets) needed for a benefit to be gained (the threshold), and you need to know if there is an upper limit over which you should not go.

Remember, in deciding the intensity you should take into account what exercise the person is already doing and their level of fitness in that component, so that you can overload appropriately.

An example of planning a safe, appropriate and effective workout to develop aerobic fitness

Suggest a safe, appropriate and effective workout for the following individual and her circumstances:

A 25-year-old woman has decided to take part in a 40km charity cycle event. At the moment, she can cycle consistently for 30 minutes. She has eight weeks to prepare.

©iStockphoto.com/clu

1. *Choose a safe and appropriate type of exercise and training method.*

The event involves cycling so the type of exercise she should do is cycling.

As it is a charity event and not a race she should use continuous steady-pace as the training method for the workout.

2. *Decide an appropriate intensity.*

She needs to be able to complete the distance but not in a set time. She should cycle at about 70% MHR. That should mean an average heart rate of around 140bpm.

3. *Decide an appropriate time/number of repetitions and sets.*

She should do a minimum of 30 minutes for her workout. Once she is capable, most of her workouts should be one hour of cycling.

An example of planning a safe, appropriate and effective workout to develop anaerobic fitness

Suggest a safe, appropriate and effective workout for the following individual and his circumstances:

A midfield hockey player wants to improve his ability to keep sprinting during a hockey match. He wants to train on the hockey pitch.

1. Choose a safe and appropriate type of exercise and training method.

Hockey involves running so the type of exercise he should use is running. Interval training (using short distances) is the most suitable training method as it matches most closely what he would be required to do in a hockey match.

2. Decide an appropriate intensity.

He should run flat-out (100% effort) repeatedly over a short distance, for example from the goal line to the end of the 'D', as this best matches what he would be required to do in hockey matches.

3. Decide an appropriate time/number of repetitions and sets.

The fixed time for the distance is not important, but working flat-out is. After each repetition he should recover by jogging back to the goal line. He should complete a set of 15 repetitions. After the first set he should complete a five-minute easy jog, then do another set of 15 repetitions.

Evaluating the safety, appropriateness and effectiveness of an aerobic or anaerobic workout

1. Judge whether a safe and appropriate *type of exercise* and *training method* were chosen for the aerobic or anaerobic workout. If you see a problem you should say what is wrong and be able to explain an appropriate alternative.

2. Judge whether an appropriate *intensity* has been selected for the aerobic or anaerobic workout. If you see a problem you should say what is wrong and be able to explain an appropriate alternative.

3. Judge whether an appropriate *time/number of repetitions and sets* has been selected for the aerobic or anaerobic workout. If you see a problem you should say what is wrong and be able to explain an appropriate alternative.

TASK 2 on Exercise/training session

Purpose

To practise planning safe, appropriate and effective workouts for developing aerobic or anaerobic fitness.

Instructions

Suggest safe, appropriate and effective workouts to develop either aerobic or anaerobic fitness for the following individuals and their circumstances:

- a health-related aerobic workout for a 40-year-old man who is overweight but not embarrassed about it. He has not exercised for many years.

- an aerobic workout for an 18-year-old girl who wants to join the army. She is reasonably fit at the moment.

- an anaerobic workout for a sprinter who can run the 200m track event in 26 seconds

To check your understanding, get other students to evaluate your attempts at planning. In return, you should evaluate their attempts.

Planning to develop muscular fitness – power, strength, speed and endurance

First consider the goal and what is expected (health-related or performance-related). Consider the gender, age, weight, body type, present level of fitness and personal preferences of the individual.

The goal and the information available on the individual should be kept in mind when making the following decisions.

1. Choose a safe and appropriate training method.

Weight training, circuit training or assault-course-type training can be used to develop health-related fitness or physical fitness for peak performance. Weight training can cover all of the muscular fitness components. Circuit training and assault-course-type training are best suited for improving muscular endurance, but can be used for the other components.

Which method you choose may well depend on the circumstances of the individual. Isometric training can be used, but it is not recommended.

2. Choose safe and appropriate exercises.

There are a wide variety of weight-training exercises. It is easy to change the weight being lifted to make weight training suitable for any component of muscular fitness.

With circuit training it is possible, but more difficult, to choose different exercises to make them harder or easier for the range of muscular fitness components. There is a similar problem with assault-course-type training, where the demands of the course have to be changed to suit the range of muscular fitness components.

3. Decide an appropriate order for the exercises.

Generally the exercises for the different parts of the body are done in rotation. For example, an exercise for the arms or chest is followed by an exercise for the trunk, which is followed by an exercise for the legs, and so on. The principle is to allow the muscles of one area to recover before they are worked again.

4. Decide an appropriate intensity for the exercises.

The tables on page 50 show the intensities to be used for the range of muscular fitness components when using weight training or circuit training. Rest/recovery times between each set are also shown.

5. Decide an appropriate number of repetitions and sets (or time).

The tables on page 50 show the number of repetitions and sets that should be used to develop the range of muscular fitness components.

Evaluating the safety, appropriateness and effectiveness of a workout to develop muscular fitness

1. Judge whether a safe and appropriate *training method* was chosen to develop the component of muscular fitness. If you see a problem you should say what is wrong and be able to explain an appropriate alternative.

2. Judge whether safe and appropriate *exercises* were chosen to develop the component of muscular fitness. If you see a problem you should say what is wrong and be able to explain an appropriate alternative.

3. Judge whether an appropriate *order* for the exercises was chosen to develop the component of muscular fitness. If you see a problem you should say what is wrong and be able to explain an appropriate alternative.

4. Judge whether an appropriate *intensity* for the exercises has been selected to develop the component of muscular fitness. If you see a problem you should say what is wrong and be able to explain an appropriate alternative.

5. Judge whether an appropriate *number of repetitions and sets* has been selected to develop the component of muscular fitness. If you see a problem you should say what is wrong and be able to explain an appropriate alternative.

▷ TASK 3 on Exercise/training session

Purpose

To build up a bank of exercises suitable for using to develop muscular fitness.

Instructions

Research and select safe and appropriate exercises to develop muscular fitness in the upper body, trunk and lower body using:

- weights as the method of training
- circuits as the method of training
- an assault course in a normal school gym as the method of training

▷ TASK 4 on Exercise/training session

Purpose

To develop your ability to plan effective workouts to develop the components of muscular fitness.

Instructions

Suggest safe, appropriate and effective workouts to develop the following components of muscular fitness:

1. Choose six safe and appropriate *weight-training exercises* to cover the major areas of the body. Write down and explain the order in which the exercises will be done. Using Repetition Maximum (RM) to represent the weight, outline and explain a workout that will effectively develop *muscular endurance.*

2. Choose six safe and appropriate *weight-training exercises* to cover the major areas of the body. Write down and explain the order in which the exercises will be done. Using a percentage of 1RM to represent the weight, outline and explain a workout that will effectively develop *muscular power.*

3. Choose six safe and appropriate *weight-training exercises* to cover the major areas of the body. Write down and explain the order in which the exercises will be done. Using RM to represent the weight, outline and explain a workout that will effectively develop *muscular speed.*

4. Choose six safe and appropriate *circuit-training exercises* (no weights) to cover the major areas of the body. The exercises should be suitable for developing *muscular endurance.* Explain your choice of exercises with regard to the *intensity*. Write down and explain the order in which the exercises will be done. Outline and explain the work time or the number of repetitions, the recovery time between each exercise, and the number of circuits to be completed.

5. Choose six safe and appropriate *circuit-training exercises* (no weights) to cover the major areas of the body. The exercises should be suitable for developing *muscular strength*. Explain your choice of exercises with regard to the *intensity*. Write down and explain the order in which the exercises will be done. Outline and explain the work time or the number of repetitions, the recovery time between each exercise, and the number of circuits to be completed.

6. An assault course is likely to involve you running, jumping and landing, swinging using a rope, and climbing. For each of these, explain how you would increase the intensity from a focus of developing *muscular endurance* to a focus of developing *muscular strength.*

Work with others and get them to evaluate your suggested workouts. In return, you should evaluate their suggestions. Discuss your findings with each other.

Planning to develop flexibility

Flexibility is an important component of fitness, but you would rarely have a specific workout for it. Flexibility exercises would normally be done as part of every exercise or training session in the warm-up, and then specially to develop flexibility in the cool-down after the pulse-lowering activity.

The cool-down is the best time to develop flexibility as the muscles are warm and pliable and can be stretched better.

The steps to follow for developing flexibility are detailed on pages 136–137.

Planning a safe, appropriate and effective cool-down

Why have a cool-down?

The purpose of a cool-down is to bring the body back to normal conditions gradually and safely.

A safe, appropriate and effective cool-down should include:

- **pulse-lowering activities**
- **flexibility exercises**
- **relaxation exercises** (optional)

The reason for including pulse-lowering activities in the cool-down is to gradually ease your way out of the strenuous exercise in the workout. By keeping exercising gently you allow:

- the build-up of waste products such as lactic acid to be broken down and cleared from the muscles
- the blood to be gradually redirected back to other internal organs
- your body temperature to decrease gradually and return to normal

The first reason for including flexibility exercises in the cool-down is to ease the tension in tight muscles as a result of the workout.

The second reason is because the cool-down is the best time to develop flexibility, as the muscles are warm and pliable and can be stretched better.

A cool-down can, if desired, be finished with relaxation exercises. These often involve tensing your muscles and then completely relaxing them. During relaxation you can listen to soothing music and be encouraged to think pleasant thoughts.

Planning the pulse-lowering activities

1. Choose a safe and appropriate pulse-lowering activity.

The pulse-lowering activity would normally be the type of aerobic exercise that you were doing in the workout. You should be able to describe the type of exercise to be done.

2. Decide on the intensity.

You should gradually lower the intensity from the level at the end of the workout towards resting level.

3. Decide on the time.

The time will depend on the individual and how hard or intense the workout was. The harder the workout, the longer the cool-down.

An example to illustrate this:

1. *Choose a safe and appropriate pulse-lowering activity*.

If you were running in your workout then you should use jogging as your pulse-lowering activity in your cool-down, as this matches what you were doing in the workout.

2. *Decide on the intensity*.

You would start jogging which is low-intensity exercise. Gradually the heart rate and body temperature will decrease and come close to resting levels.

3. *Decide on the time*. This will take between 5 to 15 minutes. The time will depend on the individual and how hard the workout was.

Planning to develop flexibility

First consider the goal and what is expected (health-related or performance-related). Consider the gender, age, weight, body type, present level of fitness and personal preferences of the individual.

The goal and the information available on the individual should be kept in mind when making the following decisions.

1. Choose a safe and appropriate training method.

You can do static flexibility exercises or ballistic/dynamic/active flexibility exercises. If you choose static flexibility you can do them passively or actively (see Section, 4 page 52). For most people and most situations, static flexibility exercises performed actively are the most appropriate.

2. Choose safe and appropriate exercises.

There are a wide range of flexibility exercises. Static flexibility exercises are normally chosen because they are safer to perform and more effective than ballistic flexibility exercises.

The static flexibility exercises should be performed actively as you are in control of the tension. If they are performed passively then another person provides the force to stretch the muscles under tension, and there is a greater risk of injury occurring. Normally you would have flexibility exercises to cover the neck, shoulders, arms, chest, trunk, hips and legs. You should be able to describe and illustrate, with the use of stick diagrams, how the flexibility exercises should be performed.

3. Decide an appropriate order for the exercises.

It is best to be systematic about the order. For example, start with the neck and work your way down the body. This helps ensure that you remember to cover all the areas of the body.

4. Decide an appropriate intensity for the exercises.

With static flexibility exercises you slowly stretch the muscle to its normal limit, then stretch it a little bit further until it is under mild tension. This is an appropriate intensity.

5. Decide an appropriate time/number of repetitions and sets.

With static flexibility exercises you should hold the muscle in the stretched position under mild tension for 5 to 10 seconds in a warm-up and for 30 to 60 seconds when developing your flexibility. Repetitions of the exercises can be performed to develop flexibility further. With ballistic flexibility exercises you would do a fixed number of repetitions, for example 20 repetitions for each exercise.

Evaluating the safety, appropriateness and effectiveness of a cool-down

1. Judge whether the cool-down includes *pulse-lowering activity* and *flexibility exercises*. If either of the two is missing you should point this out and explain why it should be included in the cool-down.

©iStockphoto.com/anirav

2. Judge whether the *pulse-lowering activity* is a safe and appropriate follow-on from the workout and whether the *intensity* and *time* are suitable for the cool-down. If you see a problem you should say what is wrong and explain an appropriate alternative.

3. Judge whether the *flexibility exercises* are safe and appropriate for developing flexibility, and whether the *intensity* and *time* provide a suitable overload to make the flexibility exercises effective. If you see a problem you should say what is wrong and explain an appropriate alternative.

An example to illustrate this:

Evaluate the use of the following exercise for developing flexibility in the cool-down.

The exercise

The purpose of using this exercise is to stretch the **gastrocnemius muscles** (the calf muscles at the back of your lower leg).

Stand on a flat floor. Slowly raise your heels up off the floor to balance on your toes. Hold this position for ten seconds, then lower your heels to the floor. Repeat.

The evaluation

First consider whether it is safe and appropriate. This exercise may be safe to perform, but it is totally inappropriate as it is not a static flexibility exercise. This exercise works or makes the gastrocnemius muscles contract instead of stretching them.

Now consider if the intensity and time are suitable. If this exercise was a static flexibility exercise used for a warm-up, and it was held under mild tension for the ten seconds as mentioned, the overload would be suitable. However, holding the stretch for ten seconds is not long enough when you wish to develop or improve flexibility as part of a cool-down.

Now demonstrate your knowledge and understanding by describing a safe and appropriate static flexibility exercise with a suitable overload. An alternative static flexibility exercise would be to stand about one metre from a wall. Reach forward and put your hands on the wall. Keeping your heels on the floor and your body straight, lean in towards the wall until you feel mild tension in your calf muscles. Hold the muscles in this stretched position under mild tension for 30 seconds.

 TASK 5 for Exercise/training session

Purpose

To build up a bank of safe and appropriate static flexibility exercises suitable for warm-ups, workouts or cool-downs, and to be able to describe and illustrate how they should be performed to make them effective.

Instructions

Research and select safe and appropriate static flexibility exercises for each of the following areas – neck, shoulders, arms, chest, trunk, hips and legs. Describe and illustrate, with the use of stick diagrams, how the exercises should be performed to make them effective.

 TASK 6 for Exercise/training session

Purpose

To be aware of flexibility exercises that are considered unsafe for warm-ups, workouts or cool-downs, and to be able to describe and illustrate why they are considered unsafe.

Instructions

Research and select flexibility exercises that are considered unsafe. Describe and illustrate, with the use of stick diagrams, why they are unsafe.

 SUMMARY

Although this section covers the exercise/training session in the order of warm-up, workout and cool-down, in planning terms the workout should be planned first as it is the main focus of the session. The warm-up is to ease you into the workout, and the cool-down (apart from developing flexibility) is to ease you out of the workout.

In this section you have learnt what steps to follow to plan safe, appropriate and effective workouts to develop aerobic and anaerobic energy production; muscular power, strength, speed and endurance; and flexibility. You have had practice in effectively applying the concepts, facts, terminology, methods and principles of training contained in previous sections.

You have also learnt how to plan safe, appropriate and effective warm-ups to ease you into the workout, and safe, appropriate and effective cool-downs to ease you out of the workout.

Section 13
Exercise/training programme

An exercise/training session on its own is not enough to develop physical fitness. Development will only occur when you have a series of sessions.

An **exercise/training programme** is a planned series of exercise/training sessions to achieve a goal over a period of time.

Planning an exercise or training programme is a bit like baking a cake. When you bake a cake, there are certain principles that you must follow, but it is possible to change some of the ingredients and to mix the ingredients in different ways in an attempt to bake a better cake. Sometimes it works and sometimes it doesn't, but people continually try to discover new or better recipes.

It is the same with planning exercise or training programmes. There are principles that you must follow, but people are continually trying out new methods and different ways of mixing the ingredients of training programmes, in the hope of discovering something that makes training more effective.

In this section the focus will be on your ability to plan exercise/training programmes which demonstrate, in a clear and straightforward manner, your ability to apply the principles of training effectively, using safe and appropriate methods of training and exercise.

Before moving on, it would be helpful to read Sections 4 and 5 again to check your understanding of them.

When the focus is on developing or maintaining health, the programme is referred to as an **exercise programme**. When the focus is on developing peak physical fitness, the programme is referred to as a **training programme**.

In planning an exercise or training programme it is the workouts that you are planning. You can assume that a warm-up and cool-down will be done with each workout.

◯ Planning a weekly health-related exercise programme

There are seven principles of training. Six of them must be applied to weekly health-related exercise programmes for them to be safe, appropriate and effective:

specificity	overload	rest/recovery
variety	progressive overload	maintenance/reversibility

Step 1: Applying the principle of specificity

Components of physical fitness

Your first decision in planning an exercise programme for health is to identify the relative importance of the seven components of physical fitness. In this case you want to identify the components that are most important for health. It is generally agreed that aerobic energy production, muscular endurance and flexibility are the most important components.

Type of exercise and training methods

The next step in applying the principle of specificity is to decide the type of exercise and training methods to be used for each component.

Aerobic energy production

As the goal is to develop fitness for health, you can choose any type of aerobic exercise that you like. You could do swimming in one session, cycling in another, rowing in another and so on, or you could do a combination of them in one session. Certain activities may be safer or better to use because of the circumstances of some individuals, otherwise the choice can be on individual preference. Continuous steady-pace training is most often used in health-related exercise programmes, but it is acceptable to include fartlek, interval or circuit training.

Muscular endurance

To develop and maintain muscular endurance you can choose a series of safe and appropriate exercises. Circuit training or weight training are methods that can be used.

Flexibility

To develop or maintain flexibility you can choose a series of static flexibility exercises that will be performed actively.

Step 2: Applying the principle of variety

Some people get bored doing the same type of exercise week in, week out. With a health-related exercise programme there is scope for including variety. As long as the type of exercise chosen develops the component of fitness, then the exercise or activity is acceptable.

Step 3: Applying the principle of overload

There is a minimum overload required on the body in order to gain a health benefit.

The following table shows the minimum overload for a health benefit to be gained in the three health-related components of physical fitness.

Activity for health	The FITT principle (minimum overload to gain a health benefit)			
	F = Frequency	I = Intensity	T = Time	T = Type of exercise
Aerobic exercise	3 sessions/week	55% or 70% MHR	20 minutes	Continuous
Muscular endurance exercise	3 sessions/week	Moderate to hard exercises with many repetitions	Cover major muscles	Weights, circuit training or exercises
Flexibility exercise	3 sessions/week	Mild tension felt in stretched muscles	Cover muscles surrounding major joints	Static flexibility exercises

If we use the FITT principle as the minimum overload, but add an upper limit to each of the variables of frequency, intensity and time, then we create a range from which we can select an appropriate overload based on the individual and their circumstances.

The table below shows an acceptable range for each of the three components of fitness.

Activity for health	The FITT principle (minimum overload to gain a health benefit)			
	F = Frequency	I = Intensity	T = Time	T = Type of exercise
Aerobic exercise	3–5 sessions/week	55–90% MHR	20–60 minutes	Continuous
Muscular endurance exercise	3–5 sessions/week	Moderate to hard exercises with many repetitions	Cover major muscles 10–60 minutes	Weights, circuit training or exercises
Flexibility exercise	3–5 sessions/week	Mild tension felt in stretched muscles	Cover muscles surrounding major joints 10–20 minutes	Static flexibility exercises

The lower end of the range would be used with individuals who are frail, perhaps obese, and who have not exercised for a long time. The upper end would be used with individuals who are in good shape and who want to be more than healthy – they want to be physically fit.

In deciding on an appropriate overload for a health-related exercise programme, you should consider the amount of aerobic, muscular endurance and flexibility exercise that the person is currently doing and their level of fitness in each. It is also worth considering the individual's age, gender and weight.

If a person is not exercising or is doing little exercise, the first priority is to get them up to the minimum overload (the lower part of the range using the FITT principle) so that a health benefit may be gained. To overload you can increase the frequency, intensity or time, or any combination of these.

Step 4: Applying the principle of progressive overload

Once you have established the initial overload at the start of the exercise programme, you can continue to progressively overload by increasing the frequency, intensity or time, or any combination of these. In health-related exercise programmes it is best to consider increasing the frequency first, followed by the time, and finally, if necessary, increasing the intensity; for health it is better to have lots of days and lots of time spent exercising at a moderate intensity, than to have fewer days and limited time spent exercising at a high intensity.

Step 5: Applying the principle of rest/recovery

You must get the correct balance between overload and rest/recovery. After periods or days of hard work there should be a rest/recovery day. This could still involve exercising, but it would be low-intensity exercise and not last too long.

If the intensity is moderate throughout the exercise programme, as is often the case in health-related exercise programmes, then rest/recovery days are not always necessary. For example, it would be possible to go walking seven days per week.

Step 6: Applying the principle of maintenance/reversibility

Once you have got your body in the condition you want, you must continue to exercise to maintain it in that condition. If you stop exercising then the biological adaptations produced by the body, and the health benefit gained from them, will be gradually lost.

The principle of peaking doesn't apply to health-related exercise programmes.

An example of planning a health-related exercise programme

The challenge is to plan a safe, appropriate and effective weekly health-related exercise programme, to take the person described below from his present state of inactivity and unfitness to being active and in a state of good physical health. Your decisions should be explained.

Profile

Des Aster is a 25-year-old male. He is single. He lives three miles from his work and travels there by bus. He works for an insurance company that provides a gym for its workers. Des has done no planned exercise for years and he has become overweight. He likes swimming and used to be quite a good swimmer. He also likes being outdoors.

The training programme has been split into two phases. The first phase is to get Des to do the minimum amount of exercise so that he can gain a health benefit. The second phase is to take him beyond this, into a state of good physical health.

PHASE 1

The intention is to have Des exercise at the minimum requirements for a health benefit to be gained.

Step 1: Applying the principle of specificity

Components of physical fitness

His exercise programme must include exercise to develop his aerobic energy production, muscular endurance and flexibility. These are the core components of any health-related exercise programme.

Type of exercise and training methods

Aerobic energy production

Swimming will definitely be in his exercise programme as he enjoys it. Swimming is also a good activity because he is overweight and his weight will be supported in the water.

There is also the possibility of using the gym at work for cycling and walking. There are future possibilities for having Des cycling or walking to or from work.

The continuous steady-pace method of training will be used.

Muscular endurance

The swimming will help develop his muscular endurance in this phase, as many of the major muscles of the arms and legs will be used in the activity. The cycling and walking will help develop the muscular endurance of the leg muscles. Exercises for core stability such as sit-ups will be included to cover the trunk, as well as other exercises for the upper and lower body.

Flexibility

The swimming will contribute towards developing his flexibility. After doing the swimming and cycling, a series of static flexibility exercises will also be performed as part of the cool-down. To develop flexibility, each stretch will be held for 20 seconds.

Step 2: Applying the principle of variety

Des likes swimming, so this is an activity that will be included in the exercise programme. In this phase cycling will also be included as an aerobic activity – his body weight is supported in cycling. He will also have muscular endurance exercises and static flexibility exercises to perform.

Step 3: Applying the principle of overload

As Des was doing no exercise at all, the overload for Week 1 will simply be to get him into the gym to do some low-intensity exercise, and to get him to complete a 15-minute continuous swim with as few breaks as possible.

The frequency, intensity and time will be below the minimum stated in the FITT principle, but this will still be an overload as he had been doing no exercise at all. He will not be put under too much stress, so he should feel fine about exercising the following week.

Step 4: Applying the principle of progressive overload

The initial overload should be appropriate, but relatively comfortable, for Des. The intention is to increase the frequency, intensity and time from Week 1, so that by Week 4 Des is doing aerobic exercise, muscular endurance exercises and flexibility exercises with the minimum overload stated in the FITT principle. Over Weeks 2–4 the frequency, intensity and time will be gradually increased until the minimum overload is reached.

A suggestion on how this could be done can be found in the table overleaf. The **bold print** shows the additional overload added week by week.

Step 5: Applying the principle of rest/recovery

In this phase there will be lots of rest/recovery time between the exercise sessions. For example, in Week 4 Sunday and Monday will be rest/recovery days; Tuesday and Wednesday will have exercise sessions; Thursday and Friday will be rest/recovery days; and Saturday will have an exercise session.

The rest/recovery days are interspersed between the exercise sessions.

Week	Sun	Mon	Tues	Wed	Thurs	Fri	Sat
1	Rest	Rest	*At gym:* **Cycle** **60% MHR** **15 mins** **Static flexibility exercises** **Hold 20 secs**	Rest	Rest	Rest	*At leisure centre:* **Swim** **60% MHR** **15 mins** **Static flexibility exercises** **Hold 20 secs**
2	Rest	Rest	*At gym:* Cycle 60% MHR **20 mins** Static flexibility exercises Hold 20 secs	*At leisure centre:* **Swim** **70% MHR** **20 mins** **Static flexibility exercises** **Hold 20 secs**	Rest	Rest	*At leisure centre:* **Weights – 2 x 20 x 25RM*** Static flexibility exercises Hold 20 secs Swim **70% MHR** 15 mins
3	Rest	Rest	*At gym:* Cycle **70% MHR** 20 mins **Weights – 2 x 20 x 25RM*** Static flexibility exercises Hold 20 secs	*At leisure centre:* Swim 70% MHR 20 mins Static flexibility exercises Hold 20 secs	Rest	Rest	*At leisure centre:* Weights – 2 x 20 x 25RM Static flexibility exercises Hold 20 secs Swim 70% MHR **20 mins**
4	Rest	Rest	*At gym:* Cycle 70% MHR 20 mins Weights – 2 x 20 x 25RM Static flexibility exercises Hold 20 secs	*At leisure centre:* **Weights – 2 x 20 x 25RM*** Static flexibility exercises Hold 20 secs Swim 70% MHR 20 mins	Rest	Rest	*At leisure centre:* Weights – 2 x 20 x 25RM Static flexibility exercises Hold 20 secs Swim 70% MHR 20 mins

* 2 x 20 x 25RM = 2 sets of 20 repetitions with a weight of 25RM

Step 6: Applying the principle of maintenance

Week 4 will have Des doing the minimum amount of exercise to gain a health benefit. If he continues with Week 4 being his weekly health-related exercise programme, he will maintain a basic level of fitness that will benefit his health.

This would be Phase 1 completed.

Phase 2 will take Des from doing the minimum amount of exercise necessary to gain a health benefit to being active and in a state of good physical health.

PHASE 2

The intention is to have Des become active and develop a state of good physical health.

Step 1: Applying the principle of specificity

Components of physical fitness

His exercise programme will still include exercise to further develop his aerobic energy production, muscular endurance and flexibility. These are the core components of any health-related exercise programme.

Types of exercise and training methods

Aerobic energy production

Swimming will definitely be maintained in his exercise programme as he enjoys it. Swimming is also a good activity because he is overweight and his weight will be supported in the water.

The gym will be used in this phase for cycling and walking. In the cycling, like the swimming, his weight is supported.

The continuous steady-pace method of training will mainly be used, but some fartlek or interval may be introduced.

Muscular endurance

The swimming will help develop the muscular endurance of the major muscles of his arms and legs. The cycling and walking will help develop the muscular endurance of his leg muscles. Weight training will be used in this phase, as a gym is available at work and at the leisure centre where he swims.

Flexibility

The swimming will help towards developing his flexibility. Also, after doing most of his workouts he will do a series of static flexibility exercises as part of his cool-down. To develop flexibility further, each stretch will be held for 30 seconds.

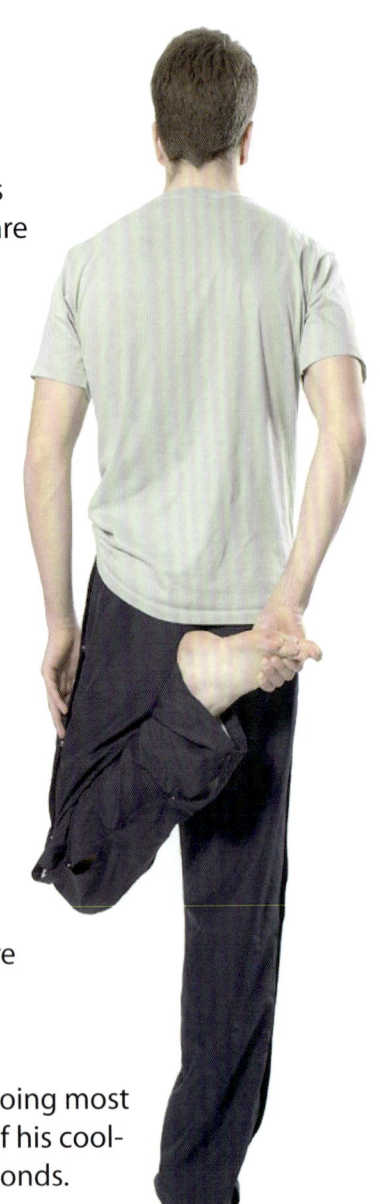

Step 2: Applying the principle of variety

Des likes swimming so this is an activity that will be maintained in the exercise programme. In this phase cycling and walking will also be included as aerobic activities – his body weight is supported in the cycling. He will do muscular endurance exercises using weights and he will continue with static flexibility exercises.

Step 3: Applying the principle of overload

Week 4 in Phase 1 is the starting point for Des in Phase 2. He will already be doing aerobic exercise, muscular endurance exercises and flexibility exercises with the minimum overload stated in the FITT principle. The principle of overload should be applied to the starting point which is shown in the table below. In this case the initial overload will be achieved by introducing an additional workout on the Friday.

Week	Sun	Mon	Tues	Wed	Thurs	Fri	Sat
	Rest	Rest	*At gym:* Cycle 70% MHR 20 mins Weights 2 x 20 x 25RM Static flexibility exercises Hold 20 secs	*At leisure centre:* Weights 2 x 20 x 25RM Static flexibility exercises Hold 20 secs Swim 70% MHR 20 mins	Rest	Rest	*At leisure centre:* Weights 2 x 20 x 25RM Static flexibility exercises Hold 20 secs Swim 70% MHR 20 mins

Step 4: Applying the principle of progressive overload

Over Weeks 5–10 the frequency, intensity or time, or a combination of these, will be gradually increased until Des is active and in a state of good physical health. This will be done by gradually increasing the frequency and time of the workouts before increasing their intensity.

A suggestion on how this would be applied can be seen in the table on the following pages. The bold print shows the additional overload added week by week.

Step 5: Applying the principle of rest/recovery

In this phase there will be less rest/recovery days between the exercise sessions, as the intention is for Des to be active. However, the balance between the exercise and the rest/recovery days should allow Des to be in a state of good physical health.

Step 6: Applying the principle of maintenance

By Week 10 Des will be quite active in that he does exercise on five days of the week. If he continues with this weekly health-related exercise programme he will maintain a state of good physical health.

Week	Sun	Mon	Tues	Wed	Thurs	Fri	Sat
5	Rest	Rest	*At gym:* Cycle 70% MHR **10 mins** **Walk** **70% MHR** **10 mins** Weights 2 x 20 x 25RM Static flexibility exercises Hold 20 secs	*At leisure centre:* Weights 2 x 20 x 25RM Static flexibility exercises **Hold 30 secs** Swim 70% MHR 20 mins	Rest	*At gym:* **Cycle** **70% MHR** **15 mins** **Walk** **70% MHR** **10 mins** **Weights** **2 x 20 x 25RM** **Static flexibility exercises** **Hold 20 secs**	*At leisure centre:* Weights 2 x 20 x 25RM Static flexibility exercises Hold 20 secs Swim 70% MHR 20 mins
6	Rest	Rest	*At gym:* Cycle 70% MHR **15 mins** Walk 70% MHR 10 mins Weights 2 x 20 x 25RM Static flexibility exercises **Hold 30 secs**	*At leisure centre:* Weights 2 x 16 x **20RM** Static flexibility exercises Hold 30 secs Swim 70% MHR 20 mins	Rest	*At gym:* Cycle 70% MHR 15 mins Walk 70% MHR 10 mins Weights 2 x 20 x 25RM Static flexibility exercises **Hold 30 secs**	*At leisure centre:* Weights 2 x 20 x 25RM Static flexibility exercises **Hold 30 secs** Swim 70% MHR **30 mins**

7	Outside: **Walk** **70% MHR** **30 mins**	Rest	At gym: Cycle 70% MHR 15 mins Walk 70% MHR 15 mins Weights 2 x 20 x 25RM Static flexibility exercises Hold 30 secs	At leisure centre: Weights 2 x 16 x 20RM Static flexibility exercises Hold 30 secs Swim 70% MHR 20 mins	Rest	At gym: Cycle 70% MHR 15 mins Walk 70% MHR **15 mins** Weights 2 x 20 x 25RM Static flexibility exercises Hold 30 secs	At leisure centre: Weights **2 x 16 x 20RM** Static flexibility exercises Hold 30 secs Swim 70% MHR **40 mins**
8	Outside: Walk 70% MHR **40 mins**	Rest	At gym: Cycle 70% MHR **20 mins** Walk 70% MHR 15 mins Weights **2 x 16 x 20RM** Static flexibility exercises Hold 30 secs	At leisure centre: Weights 2 x 16 x 20RM Static flexibility exercises Hold 30 secs Swim 70% MHR **30 mins**	Rest	At gym: Cycle 70% MHR **25 mins** Walk 70% MHR 15 mins Weights 2 x 20 x 25RM Static flexibility exercises Hold 30 secs	At leisure centre: Weights 2 x 16 x 20RM Static flexibility exercises Hold 30 secs Swim 70% MHR 40 mins

Week							
9	Outside: Walk 70% MHR **50 mins**	Rest	At gym: Cycle **70–90% MHR** **Intervals – 1 min** **fast, 1 min slow** **10 mins** Walk 70% MHR **20 mins** Weights 2 x 16 x 20RM Static flexibility exercises Hold 30 secs	At leisure centre: Weights 2 x 16 x 20RM Static flexibility exercises Hold 30 secs Swim 70% MHR 30 mins	Rest	Outside: **Walk home from** **work** **70% MHR** **< 60 mins**	At leisure centre: Weights 2 x 16 x 20RM Static flexibility exercises Hold 30 secs Swim 70% MHR 40 mins
10	Outside: Walk home from work 70% MHR **60 mins**	Rest	At gym: Cycle 70–90% MHR Intervals – 1 min fast, 1 min slow **15 mins** Walk 70% MHR 15 mins Weights 2 x 16 x 20RM Static flexibility exercises Hold 30 secs	At leisure centre: Weights 2 x 16 x 20RM Static flexibility exercises Hold 30 secs Swim 70% MHR 30 mins	Rest	Outside: Walk home from work 70% MHR < 60 mins	At leisure centre: Weights 2 x 16 x 20RM Static flexibility exercises Hold 30 secs Swim 70% MHR 40 mins

TASK 1 on Exercise/training programme

Purpose

To help you develop your ability to plan safe, appropriate and effective weekly health-related exercise programmes for a range of individuals and their circumstances.

Instructions

Demonstrate that you can plan a safe, appropriate and effective exercise programme for the following individuals and their circumstances.

1. Profile

A lady is 56 years old. She has taken early retirement from her work and so needs to be careful with her money. She lives in the country about three miles from her village. She is already pretty fit and is not overweight. She likes being outdoors.

Your challenge is to plan a safe, appropriate and effective weekly health-related exercise programme that will maintain her fitness in her retirement.

2. Profile

A female adult is 26 years old. She lives in the city and has a highly paid job. She cycled to work three days per week, but has stopped cycling as it is too dangerous and often too wet and cold. She likes variety in exercising.

Your challenge is to plan a safe, appropriate and effective weekly health-related exercise programme, that will take her from cycling three times per week to an all-round health-related exercise programme with exercise sessions on at least five days per week.

3. Make up information of your own on a number of individuals and their circumstances. Then plan safe, appropriate and effective exercise programmes for them.

Evaluating a weekly health-related exercise programme

1. Judge whether the principle of *specificity* has been applied safely and appropriately. If you see a problem you should say what is wrong and be able to explain an appropriate alternative.

2. Judge whether the principle of *variety* has been applied appropriately. If you see a problem you should say what is wrong and be able to explain an appropriate alternative.

3. Judge whether the principle of *overload* has been applied appropriately and effectively. If you see a problem you should say what is wrong and be able to explain an appropriate alternative.

4. Judge whether the principle of *progressive overload* has been applied appropriately and effectively. If you see a problem you should say what is wrong and be able to explain an appropriate alternative.

5. Judge whether the principle of *rest/recovery* has been applied appropriately and effectively. If you see a problem you should say what is wrong and be able to explain an appropriate alternative.

6. Judge whether the principle of *maintenance* has been applied appropriately and effectively, if relevant in this instance. If you see a problem you should say what is wrong and be able to explain an appropriate alternative.

TASK 2 on Exercise/training programme

Purpose

To help you develop your ability to evaluate the safety, appropriateness and effectiveness of weekly health-related exercise programmes for a range of individuals and their circumstances.

Instructions

Your challenge is to evaluate the safety, appropriateness and effectiveness of your fellow students' attempts at planning health-related exercise programmes for the individuals detailed in Task 1.

Planning a training programme to develop peak physical fitness for events, sports or positions within sports

Your potential physical fitness is affected by factors such as your age, gender, height, weight, body type, ratio of fast twitch muscle fibres to slow twitch muscle fibres, vital capacity and stroke volume. You should be aware of this when planning a training programme.

The process is the same as that for planning a weekly health-related exercise programme. It is just that you need to be more thoughtful and precise for it to be appropriate and effective.

There are seven principles of training. All seven of them must be applied to training programmes for them to be safe, appropriate and effective:

specificity	progressive overload	maintenance/reversibility
variety	rest/recovery	
overload	peaking	

Step 1: Applying the principle of specificity

Components of physical fitness

To plan an appropriate training programme for an event, sport or position within a sport, you must understand clearly the physical demands of the event, sport or position, and you must understand the seven components of physical fitness.

If you can accurately describe the physical demands placed on the performer over the duration of the performance and you understand the components of physical fitness, then you should be able to judge the relative importance of the various components. The training programme must reflect this. In other words, if aerobic energy production and muscular endurance are judged to be relatively very important for the event or sport, then most time in the training programme must be spent on developing them. The results of training are very specific, so it is important that you carry out this first step correctly.

Type of exercise and training methods

Once you know the components of fitness that need to be developed, you must choose the type of exercise and the training methods that best develop these components and that most closely match the event, sport or position. In other words, if the sport requires you to run and in so doing to alternate between aerobic and anaerobic work, then the type of exercise chosen for your training should be running, and the appropriate training method is interval training, where you would be able to alternate between aerobic and anaerobic work.

Step 2: Applying the principle of variety

In training programmes for specific events, sports or positions within a sport you must be specific with your training. For example, if the event or sport involves running and aerobic energy production, then your training must involve running and the development of aerobic energy production. You cannot provide variety in the programme by offering swimming and cycling as well as running, as these will make the training programme less effective, even though they all develop aerobic energy production.

Variety can be provided by using different training methods, using different venues for the training, training at different times, or training with different people.

Step 3: Applying the principle of overload

The whole purpose of following a training programme, in this context, is to improve your physical fitness. Improvement can only happen if you apply the principle of overload – this means working harder than you have been working before.

The amount of overload will depend on the individual and their circumstances. The most important factors to consider when deciding this is the person's present level of fitness and the amount of exercise/training that they are already doing.

You should test a person's level of fitness in the relevant components for the event or sport to establish a baseline or starting point for the training programme.

You should be able to:

- design or select tests that would be appropriate for the relevant components of fitness, and explain why they are appropriate
- describe what equipment is needed to administer the test
- describe the protocol for the test (the instructions to be given on how to do the test and the rules for the test)
- explain how the test is measured and recorded
- explain how progress can be measured through using the test regularly during the training programme

The results of the tests, together with knowing the amount of exercise the person is already doing, helps you decide on an appropriate overload to start the training programme.

The skill in applying the principle of overload is to add enough stress to make a difference and make the body adapt, but not to go over the top and add too much stress which could lead to fatigue or injury. In training for peak physical fitness you will put more stress on your body than if exercising for health.

Step 4: Applying the principle of progressive overload

Once your body adapts to the initial overload (you become fitter), you overload again, and when your body adapts to this overload you overload again. The overload can be achieved by increasing the frequency, intensity or time spent training, or by increasing any combination of these variables.

In developing peak physical fitness the intensity of the training should be much higher than for developing health, because you are working your body close to its upper limits.

Performance is important in developing peak physical fitness. It is therefore essential to monitor the progress being made during the training programme and the effectiveness of the programme. This can be done by using the tests that were used to establish the baseline before the beginning of the programme. Results can be compared and progress monitored. Adjustments can then be made to the training programme as a result of the analysis.

A person's potential fitness can be influenced by age, gender, height, weight, body type, ratio of fast twitch muscle fibres to slow twitch muscle fibres, vital capacity and stroke volume. These factors can account for performances in training.

The skill in applying the principle of progressive overload is to know *when* to add a further overload, and to know *what* form that overload should take.

Step 5: Applying the principle of rest/recovery

In developing peak physical fitness you work close to your upper limits when training. This means workouts have high intensities. The harder you work the more important it is that you get rest/recovery time. Sometimes it can be total rest, but often in training programmes to develop peak physical fitness an easy training session is instead used as the recovery.

Step 6: Applying the principle of peaking

The purpose of training is to prepare your body so that it is at its peak level of physical fitness, to allow you to perform at your very best on the day of an important competition. The principle of peaking covers the final phase prior to a competition.

In the peaking phase you perform much less work, but what work you do is at a high intensity. Then, some days before the competition you ease right off or taper off with your training. This is to allow your muscles to recover completely and your fuel stores to be full.

Step 7: Applying the principle of maintenance

If you want to maintain you level of physical fitness then you need to continue to train.

If you stop training then the biological adaptations produced by the body will be reversed and you will lose your level of physical fitness.

Applying the SMARTER principle

This principle is not part of the decision-making in planning a training programme. However, the principle plays an important role in ensuring that your decisions are appropriate and effective.

The SMARTER principle gets you to check that:

- the decisions you make are *specific*. For example, it's not enough to decide that aerobic training will be done – you must specify running using continuous steady-pace as the method of training.

- the decisions you make are *measurable*. For example, the training will involve running, using continuous steady-pace as the method of training, for 30 minutes with a heart rate of 75% MHR.

- the decisions you make are *agreed*. The person who is to follow the training programme must be aware of the decisions and agree with them.

- the decisions you make are *realistic*. The person should be capable of doing what they are asked to do in the training programme.

- the decisions you make are *time-phased*. The person will have achieved their target within a set period of time.

- the decisions you make are *exciting*. The person is more likely to carry out the training if it is exciting for them.

- the decisions you make are *recorded*. You want to have the plan recorded so that you can check on progress being made and on the effectiveness of the training programme as it is followed.

An example of planning a training programme for a specific event

Profile

A person is doing exercise three days a week – a 60-minute swim in one workout, a 60-minute cycle in another, and a 60-minute jog in another.

The person is motivated to train hard to do a 10km road race. To set a target time for the race the person does a trial 10km run and completes it in 50 minutes. Based on the trial it is agreed that a target time of 40 minutes is feasible.

The challenge

Plan a safe, appropriate and effective 12-week training programme to allow the person to meet the target time of 40 minutes for the 10km road race. Explain your decisions to convince them that the training programme will be appropriate and effective.

Week	Sun	Mon	Tues	Wed	Thurs	Fri	Sat
1	Run 5km 4:45 min/km pace 24 mins	Rest	Run 5km 4:45 min/km pace 24 mins	Rest	Run 5km 4:45 min/km pace 24 mins	Rest	Run 8km 5:00 min/km pace 40 mins
2	Run 5km 4:45 min/km 24 mins	Rest	Run 8km 5:00 min/km 40 mins	Rest	Run 5km 4:45 min/km 24 mins	Rest	Run 8km 5:00 min/km 40 mins
3	Run 5km 4:45 min/km 24 mins	Rest	Run 8km 4:45 min/km 38 mins	Run 5km 5:00 min/km 25 mins	Run 5km 4:45 min/km 24 mins	Rest	Run 8km 4:45 min/km 38 mins
4	Run 5km 4:30 min/km 23 mins	Rest	Run 8km 4:45 min/km 38 mins	Fartlek run 5km 4:30 min/km 23 mins	Run 5km 4:45 min/km 24 mins	Rest	Run 10km 4:45 min/km 48 mins
5	Run 5km 4:30 min/km 23 mins	Rest	Run 8km 4:30 min/km 36 mins	Fartlek run 5km 4:45 min/km 24 mins	Run 5km 4:30 min/km 23 mins	Rest	Run 10km 4:45 min/km 48 mins
6	Run 5km 4:15 min/km 21 mins	Rest	Run 10km 4:30 min/km 45 mins	Fartlek run 5km 4:30 min/km 23 mins	Run 8km 4:30 min/km 36 mins	Rest	Run 10km 4:30 min/km 45 mins
7	Run 5km 4:15 min/km 21 mins	Rest	Run 10km 4:30 min/km 45 mins	Fartlek run 5km 4:15 min/km 21 mins	Run 5km 4:15 min/km 21 mins	Rest	Run 15km 4:30 min/km 68 mins
8	Run 5km 4:00 min/km 20 mins	Rest	Run 10km 4:15 min/km 42 mins TRIAL	Run 5km 4:15 min/km 21 mins	Run 5km 4:00 min/km 20 mins	Rest	Run 15km 4:30 min/km 68 mins
9	Run Intervals 5 x 1km 3:30 min/km Rest – 3 mins	Rest	Run Intervals 5 x 1km 3:30 min/km Rest – 3 mins	Run 5km 4:00 min/km 20 mins	Run 10km 4:30 min/km 45 mins	Rest	Run 10km 4:15 min/km 42 mins
10	Run 6 x 1km 3:30 min/km Rest – 3 mins	Rest	Run 6 x 1km 3:30 min/km Rest – 3 mins	Run 5km 4:00 min/km 20 mins	Run 10km 4:30 min/km 45 mins	Rest	Run 10km 4:15 min/km 42 mins
11	Run 5km 3:30 min/km 18 mins	Rest	Run 6 x 1km 3:30 min/km Rest – 3 mins	Run 6 x 1km 3:30 min/km Rest – 3 mins	Rest	Rest	Run 10km 4:15 min/km 42 mins
12	Run 7km 4:30 min/km 31 mins	Rest	Run 5km 4:00 min/km 20 mins	Rest	Run 4km easy 4:30 min/km 18 mins	Rest	10km RACE 4:00 min/km 40 mins

Explanation for decisions

Step 1: Applying the principle of specificity

Components of physical fitness

The 10km run will involve running at a steady pace for 40 minutes. Most energy will therefore be supplied by the aerobic energy production system. This means that this component of fitness is very important, and so most emphasis should be placed on developing it in the training programme. Anaerobic energy production is of some importance.

Local muscular endurance will be very important, especially in the legs, so this importance must be reflected in the training programme. Muscular power, strength, and speed are less important, but some work on strength/endurance would help. Flexibility will be of some importance.

Type of exercise and training methods

The aerobic energy system should be developed through running as this matches the event – 10km road race. Continuous steady-pace, fartlek and interval training would all be useful in the training programme. Local muscular endurance will also be developed through running. Some hill work or weights would help develop muscular strength/endurance. For example, the fartlek runs could be done using hills.

Step 2: Applying the principle of variety

This training programme is for a specific event so the training must be specific. It would not be appropriate to provide variety in the programme by offering swimming and cycling as well as running, as these would make the training programme less effective, even though they all develop aerobic energy production. Variety will instead be provided by using different training methods, using different venues for the training, training at different times, or training with different people.

Step 3: Applying the principle of overload

The person has already been exercising three times a week and for an hour at a time, so they should have a foundation of aerobic fitness. One of the workouts was jogging for one hour, so they should be capable of completing a 10km run. The focus of the training will be to reduce the time to run 10km from 50 to 40 minutes. The initial overload is based on this information, plus the fact that they did a 10km road trial in a time of 50 minutes.

In Week 1 of the training programme, four workouts of running are planned. This adds an additional session. Half the race distance is used for three of the workouts, but at a faster pace than the person ran in the 10km trial. The shorter distance is to allow the person to get used to changing all the workouts to running. The faster pace is to ensure that there is an overload. One longer run is included at the pace at which the trial was run (5 min/km pace).

Week	Sun	Mon	Tues	Wed	Thurs	Fri	Sat
1	Run 5km 4:45 min/km pace 24 mins	Rest	Run 5km 4:45 min/km pace 24 mins	Rest	Run 5km 4:45 min/km pace 24 mins	Rest	Run 8km 5:00 min/km pace 40 mins

Enough stress or overload has been given to make a difference to the person and make their body adapt, but it is not over the top by adding too much stress which could lead to fatigue or injury. This principle is then applied over the training programme.

Week	Sun	Mon	Tues	Wed	Thurs	Fri	Sat
1	Run 5km 4:45 min/km pace 24 mins	Rest	Run 5km 4:45 min/km pace 24 mins	Rest	Run 5km 4:45 min/km pace 24 mins	Rest	Run 8km 5:00 min/km pace 40 mins
2	Run 5km 4:45 min/km 24 mins	Rest	Run 8km 5:00 min/km 40 mins	Rest	Run 5km 4:45 min/km 24 mins	Rest	Run 8km 5:00 min/km 40 mins
3	Run 5km 4:45 min/km 24 mins	Rest	Run 8km 4:45 min/km 38 mins	Run 5km 5:00 min/km 25 mins	Run 5km 4:45 min/km 24 mins	Rest	Run 8km 4:45 min/km 38 mins

Step 4: Applying the principle of progressive overload

Progressive overload is applied in a number of ways over the training programme. Over the first three weeks a foundation is built. In Week 1 there are four workouts, with three of them requiring a higher intensity (pace) than the 10km trial and the other workout at the same pace as the trial. In Week 2 slightly more kilometres are run. In Week 3 an extra workout is added and the intensity is higher in the longer runs.

In Week 4 the intensity is increased in two out of the three shorter runs, and one of these runs is a fartlek run where bursts of speed are introduced. The longer runs stay at the same pace as Week 3. Week 5 increases the intensity in the 8km run and 5km run on Tuesday and Thursday. The fartlek run on Wednesday is easier to allow for recovery. The two other workouts in Week 5 remain the same.

Week	Sun	Mon	Tues	Wed	Thurs	Fri	Sat
4	Run 5km 4:30 min/km 23 mins	Rest	Run 8km 4:45 min/km 38 mins	Fartlek run 5 km 4:30 min/km 23 mins	Run 5km 4:45 min/km 24 mins	Rest	Run 10km 4:45 min/km 48 mins
5	Run 5km 4:30 min/km 23 mins	Rest	Run 8km 4:30 min/km 36 mins	Fartlek run 5 km 4:45 min/km 24 mins	Run 5km 4:30 min/km 23 mins	Rest	Run 10km 4:45 min/km 48 mins

Weeks 6–8 build up the number of kilometres run and keep the intensity high. It is during this phase that the race pace of 4 min/km is demanded in the shorter runs. The high intensity with the high-kilometre runs make this phase hard work. In Week 8, a 10km trial takes place with the target of running it at 4:15 min/km pace.

Week	Sun	Mon	Tues	Wed	Thurs	Fri	Sat
6	Run 5km 4:15 min/km 21 mins	Rest	Run 10km 4:30 min/km 45 mins	Fartlek run 5 km 4:30 min/km 23 mins	Run 8km 4:30 min/km 36 mins	Rest	Run 10km 4:30 min/km 45 mins
7	Run 5km 4:15 min/km 21 mins	Rest	Run 10km 4:30 min/km 45 mins	Fartlek run 5 km 4:15 min/km 21 mins	Run 5km 4:15 min/km 21 mins	Rest	Run 15km 4:30 min/km 68 mins
8	Run 5km 4:00 min/km 20 mins	Rest	Run 10km 4:15 min/km 42 mins TRIAL	Run 5km 4:15 min/km 21 mins	Run 5km 4:00 min/km 20 mins	Rest	Run 15km 4:30 min/km 68 mins

In Weeks 9–11 the emphasis is on getting used to running faster than the race pace of 4 min/km. Two workouts of interval training are added in Week 9 to introduce running at 3:30 min/km pace (5 x 1km at 3:30 min/km pace). Interval training is maintained in Weeks 10 and 11 for this high-intensity work. Short runs are at race pace or faster. The longer run is reduced from 15km to 10km.

This is one example to show the application of the principle of progressive overload. It is possible to have different combinations of the types of training used, the intensities of the various workouts, and the times expected for the workouts, as well as the frequency of sessions per week.

Week	Sun	Mon	Tues	Wed	Thurs	Fri	Sat
9	Run Intervals 5 x 1km 3:30 min/km Rest – 3 mins	Rest	Run Intervals 5 x 1km 3:30 min/km Rest – 3 mins	Run 5km 4:00 min/km 20 mins	Run 10km 4:30 min/km 45 mins	Rest	Run 10km 4:15 min/km 42 mins
10	Run 6 x 1km 3:30 min/km Rest – 3 mins	Rest	Run 6 x 1km 3:30 min/km Rest – 3 mins	Run 5km 4:00 min/km 20 mins	Run 10km 4:30 min/km 45 mins	Rest	Run 10km 4:15 min/km 42 mins
11	Run 5km 3:30 min/km 18 mins	Rest	Run 6 x 1km 3:30 min/km Rest – 3 mins	Run 6 x 1km 3:30 min/km Rest – 3 mins	Rest	Rest	Run 10km 4:15 min/km 42 mins

Step 5: Applying the principle of rest/recovery

At the start of the training programme there are three days of total rest/recovery that are spread out among the training days. As the body gets used to the training the rest/recovery days are reduced to two. These days follow two days of hard work on Saturday and Sunday and two or three days of hard work on Tuesday, Wednesday and Thursday. Sometimes the mid-week days are all hard work, but usually one allows for some recovery.

Step 6: Applying the principle of peaking

Weeks 11 and 12 count as the peaking phase. In Week 11 there is one high-intensity workout, and then a day to recover. Then there are two high-intensity workouts followed by two days to recover. In Week 12 the training tapers off to allow the muscles to recover completely from the training and the fuel stores to be full.

Week	Sun	Mon	Tues	Wed	Thurs	Fri	Sat
11	Run 5km 3:30 min/km 18 mins	Rest	Run 6 x 1km 3:30 min/km Rest – 3 mins	Run 6 x 1km 3:30 min/km Rest – 3 mins	Rest	Rest	Run 10km 4:15 min/km 42 mins
12	Run 7km 4:30 min/km 31 mins	Rest	Run 5km 4:00 min/km 20 mins	Rest	Run 4km easy 4:30 min/km 18 mins	Rest	10km RACE 4:00 min/km 40 mins

Step 7: Applying the principle of maintenance

If the person wants to maintain their level of physical fitness they need to continue to train.

If they stop training then the biological adaptations produced by the body will be reversed and they will lose their level of physical fitness.

Applying the SMARTER principle

The SMARTER principle allows you to check that:

- the decisions you make are *specific*. In this training programme the answer is yes. The person is informed about what type of exercise and what training methods should be used.

- the decisions you make are *measurable*. In this training programme the answer is yes. The person knows the distance to be run, the pace of the run and the final time for the run. In the interval workouts they know the distance, the work time, the recovery time and the number of repetitions.

- the decisions you make are *agreed*. You have explained your decisions and hopefully this will bring agreement.

- the decisions you make are *realistic*. It was initially agreed that the target time was feasible. The training has been progressively overloaded to allow the target to be reached.

- the decisions are *time-phased*. There is a 12-week training programme planned to achieve the target.

- the decisions you make are *exciting*. Knowing that the training is preparing the person to achieve the target time will be exciting for them and help keep them motivated.

- the decisions you make are *recorded*. The training programme is written down. The person should keep a record of what training is actually done each week. This can be compared to what was planned. This allows progress to be monitored and changes to be made to the training programme as necessary.

The training programme above is just one example to show how the principles of training can be applied to an individual and their circumstances to achieve a set goal for an event. It is possible to plan it in other ways and include different ingredients and have different mixes within the training programme. Whatever training programme you plan, you must be able to argue your case based on the sound application of the principles of training.

The best way to understand this and to become competent at planning training programmes is to experience the whole process yourself – in other words, to plan a training programme for yourself, implement it, monitor it, and finally evaluate it. Carrying out this whole process will not only help you prepare for the examination component, but it will also be of great help in preparing you for the component on the analysis and improvement of your own exercise profile.

TASK 3 on Exercise/training programme

Purpose
To help you develop your ability to plan safe, appropriate and effective training programmes for a range of individuals and their circumstances.

Instructions
Demonstrate that you can plan a safe, appropriate and effective aerobic training programme for yourself to achieve a set target.

Follow the steps explained in this section, but make them appropriate for yourself and your target.

Progressive overload

It is reasonably straightforward to apply the principles of specificity, initial overload, variety, rest/recovery, peaking and maintenance/reversibility appropriately and effectively to any component of physical fitness in a training programme. It is more challenging to apply the principle of progressive overload, as it is applied differently to each of the components of fitness.

How to apply the principle of progressive overload to aerobic and anaerobic energy production workouts

In Section 4 you learnt how various training methods can be used to develop either aerobic or anaerobic energy production.

For information on how interval training can be used to develop aerobic or anaerobic energy production, see the relevant parts of the table in Section 4, pages 43–45.

Aerobic energy production

To develop aerobic energy production by applying the principle of progressive overload to workouts you would:

- increase the number of repetitions or sets as your body adapts to the stress of the training
- decrease the recovery time between each repetition as your body adapted to the stress of the training
- increase the distance or work time as your body adapts to the stress of the training

If you started with an initial overload of 10 repetitions of 200m, with each repetition to be run in 40 seconds and a recovery time of 40 seconds between each repetition, then as the body adapts to this overload you could overload again by adding on more repetitions. You could then decrease the recovery time between each repetition, and finally you could increase the distance or work time.

For example:

10 reps x 200m x 40 secs x 40 secs recovery. As the body adapts to this, it could change to:

15 reps x 200m x 40 secs x 40 secs recovery. As the body adapts to this, it could change to:

20 reps x 200m x 40 secs x 40 secs recovery. As the body adapts to this, it could change to:

20 reps x 200m x 40 secs x 30 secs recovery. As the body adapts to this, it could change to:

20 reps x 200m x 40 secs x 20 secs recovery. As the body adapts to this, it could change to:

10 reps x 400m x 80 secs x 60 secs recovery. As the body adapts to this, it could change to:

15 reps x 400m x 80 secs x 60 secs recovery.

Anaerobic energy production

To develop anaerobic energy production by applying the principle of progressive overload to workouts you would:

- increase the intensity as your body adapts to the stress of the training
- increase the number of repetitions as your body adapts to the stress of the training
- decrease the recovery time between each repetition as your body adapts to the stress of the training
- increase the distance or work time as your body adapts to the stress of the training

If you started with an initial overload of 5 repetitions of 200m, with each repetition to be run in 30 seconds and a recovery time of 3 minutes between each repetition, then as the body adapts to this overload you could overload again by decreasing the time in which the distance has to be completed. You could then decrease the recovery time between each repetition, and finally you could increase the distance or work time.

For example:

5 reps x 200m x 30 secs x 3 mins recovery. As the body adapts to this, it could change to:

5 reps x 200m x 29 secs x 3 mins recovery. As the body adapts to this, it could change to:

5 reps x 200m x 28 secs x 3 mins recovery. As the body adapts to this, it could change to:

6 reps x 200m x 28 secs x 3 mins recovery. As the body adapts to this, it could change to:

7 reps x 200m x 28 secs x 3 mins recovery. As the body adapts to this, it could change to:

7 reps x 200m x 28 secs x 2:30 mins recovery. As the body adapts to this, it could change to:

7 reps x 200m x 28 secs x 2 mins recovery.

How to apply the principle of progressive overload to muscular fitness workouts

In Section 4 you learnt how various training methods can be used to develop muscular power, strength, endurance or speed.

The tables on page 50 show how weight training and circuit training can be used to develop these components of muscular fitness.

Muscular power

To develop muscular power by applying the principle of progressive overload to workouts you would:

- increase the intensity as your body adapts to the stress of the training
- increase the number of sets as your body adapts to the stress of the training

If you started with an initial overload for a particular exercise of 50kg, which was for you 5RM, and you lifted this weight for 2 sets of 3 repetitions in your workouts, then as the body adapts and you are able to lift the 50kg for 2 sets of 5 repetitions, you would increase the weight to, for example, 55kg which would keep the weight heavy at around 5RM.

For example:

2 sets of 3 repetitions with 50kg and 4 mins recovery between the sets. As the body adapts to this, it could change to:

2 sets of 3 repetitions with 55kg and 4 mins recovery between the sets. As the body adapts to this, it could change to:

2 sets of 3 repetitions with 60kg and 4 mins recovery between the sets. As the body adapts to this, it could change to:

3 sets of 3 repetitions with 60kg and 4 mins recovery between the sets.

Muscular strength

To develop muscular strength by applying the principle of progressive overload to workouts you would:

- increase the intensity as your body adapts to the stress of the training
- increase the number of sets as your body adapts to the stress of the training

If you started with an initial overload for a particular exercise of 40kg, which was for you 10RM, and you lifted this weight for 2 sets of 7 repetitions in your workouts, then as the body adapts and you are able to lift the 40kg for 2 sets of 10 repetitions, you would increase the weight to, for example, 45kg which would keep the weight heavy at around 10RM.

For example:

2 sets of 7 repetitions with 40kg and 2 mins recovery between the sets. As the body adapts to this, it could change to:

2 sets of 7 repetitions with 45kg and 2 mins recovery between the sets. As the body adapts to this, it could change to:

2 sets of 7 repetitions with 50kg and 2 mins recovery between the sets. As the body adapts to this, it could change to:

3 sets of 7 repetitions with 50kg and 2 mins recovery between the sets.

Muscular endurance

To develop muscular endurance by applying the principle of progressive overload to workouts you would:

- increase the number of repetitions as your body adapts to the stress of the training
- decrease the recovery time between sets
- increase the intensity as your body adapts to the stress of the training

If you started with an initial overload for a particular exercise of 20kg, which was for you 20RM, and you lifted this weight for 2 sets of 15 repetitions in your workouts, then as the body adapts and you are able to lift the 20kg for 2 sets of 25 repetitions, you would decrease the recovery time between the sets until you are able to do all 50 repetitions in one set.

For example:

2 sets of 15 repetitions with 20kg and 60 secs recovery between the sets. As the body adapts to this, it could change to:

2 sets of 20 repetitions with 20kg and 60 secs recovery between the sets. As the body adapts to this, it could change to:

2 sets of 25 repetitions with 20kg and 60 secs recovery between the sets. As the body adapts to this, it could change to:

2 sets of 25 repetitions with 20kg and 30 secs recovery between the sets. As the body adapts to this, it could change to:

1 set of 50 repetitions with 20kg.

Muscular speed

To develop muscular speed by applying the principle of progressive overload to workouts you would:

- increase the number of repetitions as your body adapts to the stress of the training
- increase the intensity as your body adapts to the stress of the training

If you started with an initial overload for a particular exercise of 10kg, which was for you 50RM, and you lifted this weight for 2 sets of 15 repetitions in your workouts, then as the body adapts and you are able to lift the 10kg for 2 sets of 25 repetitions, you would increase the weight to, for example, 15kg which would keep the weight at around 50RM.

For example:

2 sets of 15 repetitions with 10kg and 4 mins recovery between the sets. As the body adapts to this, it could change to:

2 sets of 20 repetitions with 10kg and 4 mins recovery between the sets. As the body adapts to this, it could change to:

2 sets of 25 repetitions with 10kg and 4 mins recovery between the sets. As the body adapts to this, it could change to:

2 sets of 15 repetitions with 15kg and 4 mins recovery between the sets.

How to apply the principle of progressive overload to flexibility

In Section 4 you learnt how various training methods can be used to develop flexibility.

With static flexibility exercises you hold the muscle in the stretched position under mild tension for 30 to 60 seconds. Over time the muscle becomes more flexible and allows a greater range of movement at the joint. If you continue to stretch the muscle as described above, flexibility will develop further and you will have an even greater range of movement at the joint.

Evaluating the safety, appropriateness and effectiveness of training programmes

1. Judge whether the principle of *specificity* has been applied safely and appropriately. If you see a problem you should say what is wrong and be able to explain an appropriate alternative.

2. Judge whether the principle of *variety* has been applied appropriately. If you see a problem you should say what is wrong and be able to explain an appropriate alternative.

3. Judge whether the principle of *overload* has been applied appropriately and effectively. If you see a problem you should say what is wrong and be able to explain an appropriate alternative.

4. Judge whether the principle of *progressive overload* has been applied appropriately and effectively. If you see a problem you should say what is wrong and be able to explain an appropriate alternative.

5. Judge whether the principle of *rest/recovery* has been applied appropriately and effectively. If you see a problem you should say what is wrong and be able to explain an appropriate alternative.

6. Judge whether the principle of *peaking* has been applied appropriately and effectively. If you see a problem you should say what is wrong and be able to explain an appropriate alternative.

7. Judge whether the principle of *maintenance* has been applied appropriately and effectively, if relevant in this instance. If you see a problem you should say what is wrong and be able to explain an appropriate alternative.

8. Judge whether the *SMARTER principle* has been applied to the training programme.

 ## TASK 4 on Exercise/training programme

Purpose

To help you develop your ability to evaluate the safety, appropriateness and effectiveness of training programmes for a range of individuals and their circumstances.

Instructions

Demonstrate that you can evaluate the safety, appropriateness and effectiveness of suggested training programmes for a range of individuals and their circumstances.

1. Share your attempts at planning training programmes for yourself or for others with fellow students, and get them to evaluate the programmes and provide you with feedback.

2. Evaluate your fellow students' attempts at planning training programmes and provide feedback to them.

 ## SUMMARY

In this section you have learnt how to apply the principles of specificity, variety, overload, progressive overload, rest/recovery, peaking and maintenance to plan health-related exercise programmes and to training programmes to develop one or more of the components of physical fitness.

You have also learnt how to evaluate whether these principles of training have been applied safely, appropriately and effectively to suggested health-related exercise programmes or suggested training programmes to develop one or more of the components of physical fitness.

Section 14

Workout for developing skills

©iStockphoto.com/barsik

In Sections 12 and 13 you learnt how to plan exercise or training sessions and programmes to develop physical fitness.

In this section you will learn how to plan safe, appropriate and effective workouts to develop the skills in sports.

The best way to learn how to do this is to practise planning workouts using the principles and methods covered in this section and in Section 10. Before moving on, read Section 10 again to check your understanding of its content.

Try planning and implementing workouts to develop various skills and get other students to evaluate your attempts. In return, you should evaluate their attempts. You also need to help each other in observing and recording each others' performances and in providing feedback to each other. This will be your task at the end of the section.

◯ Planning a safe, appropriate and effective workout to develop skills

An exercise session normally includes:

- a warm-up
- a workout
- a cool-down

This applies to health-related exercise sessions, to training sessions to develop peak physical fitness, and to sessions to develop skills.

The workout can include a conditioning phase when training is done to develop one or more of the seven components of physical fitness. This phase may be followed or preceded by a phase that develops skill, or the workout can be solely dedicated to developing skills.

In this section you will focus on the workout, or phase of the workout, that will develop skills.

Intention of the workout

It is important that you have a clear objective for the workout.

Your objective should be based on the assessment and analysis of previous performances in the sport. This allows you to identify strengths and weaknesses in the range and mastery of skills. If you are serious about improving your overall performance, then your intention in the workouts will be to develop new skills or to work on eliminating areas of weakness in other skills.

If you don't have clear intentions or objectives for your workouts, then it can be very easy for you to remain in your comfort zone and only practise your strengths.

Assessment of performance of an identified skill

To judge how well a skill is performed you must know the **'full marks' model**, in other words the sequence of movements that allows the skill to be performed efficiently, effectively and with accuracy. This covers **positioning**, **technique**, **timing** and **recovery**. If you have a clear understanding of the 'full marks' model then you can compare any performance of the skill against it and judge how well the skill has been performed. From your observations you will be able to identify areas of weakness in the performance of the skill.

It is through the observation that you judge how well a skill is being performed. Observations can be live, in that you watch the skill being performed in front of you. In this situation you need to be able to remember accurately what you saw being performed and be able to compare it to the 'full marks' model, in order to identify strengths and weaknesses in the performance. It is not always wise to judge a performance on one attempt, so many attempts should be performed and your judgement based on the patterns observed.

It is helpful if performances are recorded. This can be done using digital camcorders. You still make your judgement based on observation, but you are able to observe one performance many times or a number of different performances many times before you make a judgement. Another advantage in recording performances is that you can observe your own performances and make your own judgements based on your observations.

There are also software programmes that will allow you to analyse recorded performances and to compare one performance with another.

You cannot observe yourself perform live, but you can *feel* how well a skill was performed. This is a kinaesthetic sense. With quality practice you get the 'feel' of the 'full marks' model, and with experience you can compare what you did with this model and be able to identify your strengths and weaknesses. This feeling of performing a skill well or less well is an important part in the mastery of learning a skill.

Teaching/coaching a skill

To teach a skill you must have a thorough understanding of the 'full marks' model. You then have to be able to communicate this to a learner. This can be done visually, verbally or manually.

Visual guidance is when you demonstrate or get someone else to demonstrate the technique to be performed. The demonstration can also be done by using a video or DVD clip or by using photographs.

Verbal guidance is when you tell the learner what to do. It should be kept simple and short, especially during the cognitive stage. At all times the language should be clear, concise and consistent in the use of words.

Physical or **manual guidance** is when you physically or manually take the learner through the sequence of movements.

The most appropriate method depends on the skill. For example, basic skills can usually be demonstrated and learnt quickly from a demonstration. Complex skills need to be broken down into parts and a combination of visual and verbal guidance is usually most successful. Sometimes, even with clear visual and verbal guidance the learner still has difficulty and may need manual guidance.

The most appropriate method also depends on the learner. People usually have a predominant learning style or preferred way of processing information. For example, some people learn best with visual guidance, some with verbal guidance, and some with physical/manual guidance. Some learn best by doing or experiencing – these are **kinaesthetic learners**. Some are **analytic learners** – whether they see, hear or try the skill they need to think about it, retry it, think about it again, and so on.

Your challenge is to use your visual and verbal guidance to give the learner a mental image of how to perform the correct technique of the skill (the 'full marks' model). You then provide the learner with opportunities to demonstrate to you the correct technique without being under any pressure. You observe the learner's performances and provide feedback. The learner is then given further opportunities to demonstrate to you the correct technique of the skill. Once there is sufficient grasp of the technique, it can be performed in selected practices.

Selection of practices

The techniques for performing most skills are the same for beginners, improvers or advanced performers. All strive to perform the skill using the 'full marks' model.

The type and difficulty of the practice used depends on the complexity of the skill and on the stage that an individual is at in learning it.

Practices must suit the stage of learning. It is through quality practice of a skill over and over again an individual is able to progress through the stages of learning.

Cognitive stage

See Section 10, page 100, for information on this stage.

Practices, at this stage, should be simple with little pressure being put on the learner. The practice should allow at least a 70% success rate. Any of the types of practice could be used, but one type that illustrates what would be suitable at this stage is fixed or drill practice.

Associative stage

See Section 10, page 100, for information on this stage.

Practices, at this stage, can put some pressure on the learner and be closer to what will be required in a competitive situation. There is greater emphasis in performing the technique efficiently and effectively. The practice should allow a success rate of around 70%. Any of the types of practice could be used, but one type that illustrates what would be suitable at this stage is whole-part-whole practice.

Autonomous stage

See Section 10, page 101, for information on this stage.

Practices, at this stage, can be complex and put the learner under pressure. There is a greater emphasis on accuracy. It is expected that the technique will be performed efficiently and effectively. The practice should allow a success rate of around 70%. Any of the types of practice could be used, but one type that illustrates what would be suitable at this stage is problem-solving practice.

Giving feedback

You need to give regular and appropriate feedback on the performances of the skill.

There are two categories of extrinsic feedback:

- knowledge of results
- knowledge of performance

Knowledge of performance provides the most helpful feedback.

For this, you must provide or be provided with feedback on:

- what parts of the technique are being performed well
- what parts of the technique are being performed less well

Feedback can be visual, verbal, manual or from your intrinsic 'feelings'.

Visual feedback is when you show the learner how they are performing the technique. This can be done personally or with the use of recordings of the person performing. You then demonstrate or get someone else to demonstrate how the technique should be performed. This demonstration can be done by using a video or DVD clip.

Verbal feedback is when you tell the learner what they are doing well and what they are doing less well. This should be kept straightforward and direct. The language should always be clear, concise and consistent in the use of words. You then tell the person how the technique should be performed.

Visual and verbal feedback are usually combined to provide information on performances.

Physical or **manual feedback** is when you physically or manually take the learner through the sequence of movements to show how they were performing the skill. You then physically or manually take them through the sequence of movements as they should be performing it.

You can use your own intrinsic (internal) feedback. This provides information on the 'feel' of performing the sequence of movements. You can feel what was wrong in the performances.

Whether the feedback is intrinsic, manual, verbal or visual, the whole point in providing it is to reinforce what is good and to highlight what is less good, so that corrective actions may be taken to improve technique.

Once you have sound technique in place, practice is important. It is practising a skill using sound technique that develops and forms a clear and precise memory of the skill.

Organisation

It is important that when you have a number of people of varying abilities and stages of development together, you manage them well. If you are playing in a competitive situation it is important to match people of similar abilities or stages of learning together. This will mean that the competition should be fair and close.

However, this is not the case when providing quality practice for an individual in the cognitive or early associative stages. If matched with someone at a similar stage of development, neither person will have the control necessary to provide quality feed for the other. If someone at the autonomous stage is instead used to feed someone in the cognitive or associative stage, then they have the control to provide the person with whatever feed they require, thus allowing quality practice to take place.

To provide quality feed a person should be able to consistently place the shuttlecock in the correct area of the court with the appropriate height, so that the learner can consistently practise the selected shot.

Time is not limitless for the development and practice of skills. It needs to be managed to get effective use from it. Within the part of a workout dedicated to developing skill, you may have to include, for example:

- an explanation of the intention of the workout – 2 minutes
- an assessment of the performance of a selected skill – 5 minutes
- analysis and feedback on the performances of the skill – 5 minutes
- teaching or coaching the technique of the skill – 10 minutes
- practising the technique using selected practices with feedback on the performances of the skill – 20 minutes
- application of the skill in a competitive situation – 15 minutes
- feedback on the performances of the skill – 3 minutes

The times given above provide one example of how a 60-minute workout on a selected skill may be managed. How the time is divided up will depend on the stage of development that an individual is at, and on the type of practices to be used.

An example of planning a workout to develop skill

Profile

A teenage girl, Mary, has been playing badminton with a friend who plays for the local club.

The problem is that Mary cannot perform a forehand overhead clearance shot effectively. At best the shuttlecock only goes as far as the mid-court and her friend can easily smash this. Mary wants to learn to play properly.

Intention of the workout

Based on the observation and analysis of Mary's performances in playing competitive badminton, the forehand overhead clear was identified as a weakness.

The objective of the workout is therefore for her to be able to perform this shot with sound technique in a competitive situation.

Assessment of performance of an identified skill

The forehand overhead clear has been identified as a weakness. Mary is asked to continuously play this shot in a practice situation.

Her performances are recorded using a digital camcorder.

Her positioning, technique, timing and recovery in playing the shot are compared to the 'full marks' model.

It is noted that:

- her shoulders are nearly always parallel with the net when she plays the shot
- she plays the shot with a straight arm and has no wrist action

Mary is given the opportunity to watch the recording of her performances. As she is only starting to get taught/coached there is no point in highlighting her faults or weaknesses at this time.

Teaching/coaching the skill

Mary is given the opportunity to watch a video recording of the forehand overhead clear being performed in accordance with the 'full marks' model. The video is officially produced by the governing body of the sport.

The following points are highlighted visually and explained verbally:

- the grip to allow the wrist action
- the shoulder turn in preparation for playing the shot
- the stepping in to play the shot
- the throwing action of the arm
- the wrist action

Mary demonstrates that she can perform these actions without a shuttlecock or being in a game or using a practice. Her demonstrations are recorded and played back to her. Visual and verbal feedback is given to her. Corrective actions are then applied to areas of weakness. Mary's performances are recorded again and played back to her. Further corrective actions are taken, if necessary.

Selection of practices

Mary is in the cognitive stage, as she is learning or re-learning to play the forehand overhead clear.

The practices used are straightforward and match her stage of learning.

Practice 1

A feeder provides a high serve to land mid- to rear-court. Mary positions herself and plays a forehand overhead clear with sound technique so that the shuttlecock goes to the rear of the feeder's court. The shuttlecock is allowed to drop to the floor.

Practice 2

A feeder provides a high serve to land mid- to rear-court. Mary positions herself and plays a forehand overhead clear with sound technique so that the shuttlecock goes to the rear of the feeder's court. The feeder returns the shuttlecock to the rear of Mary's court. Both continue to play forehand overhead clearance shots to each other.

Practice 3

This takes the form of a conditioned game of badminton.

These practices can be adjusted to make them a little less or a little more challenging.

Giving feedback

Feedback is given to Mary as she demonstrates the correct technique for playing the forehand overhead clear.

Mary's performances are recorded and used for feedback. Feedback is given both during and after the three practices.

The following points will be observed specifically for Mary:

- the grip to allow the wrist action
- the shoulder turn in preparation for playing the shot
- the stepping in to play the shot
- the throwing action of the arm
- the wrist action

Visual and verbal feedback are provided on:

- what parts of the technique are being performed well
- what parts of the technique are being performed less well

The feedback is used to reinforce what is good and to highlight what is less good, so that corrective actions may be taken to improve technique.

Organisation

For all the practices (1, 2 and 3) it is necessary to have someone who can consistently feed the shuttlecock accurately to the appropriate area of the court. This will allow Mary to consistently practise the forehand overhead clear.

If the workout was to last 30 minutes, then the timings for the various parts of the workout could be as follows:

- an explanation of the intention of the workout – 1 minute
- an assessment of the performance – 3 minutes
- teaching or coaching the 'full marks' technique of the skill and giving feedback – 5 minutes
- practising the technique using the three practices with feedback on the performances of the skill – 20 minutes
- Summing up – 1 minute

It is known that Mary's forehand overhead clear is a weakness. The intention of the workout is therefore to address this weakness. The three minutes demonstrating the shot gives time for an analysis to be made of the shot and for faults in the technique to be identified. Mary is to learn the technique of the forehead overhead clear, so the five minutes is spent checking that she can demonstrate the technique correctly. The shot is then practised in isolation, one shot at a time as in Practice 1. If the performances are consistently sound in this practice, it is possible for Mary to move on to Practice 2, where a continuous rally using forehand overhead clears is maintained. Again, if the performances are consistently sound in this practice, it is possible to move on to Practice 3. Practice 3 allows a range of shots to be used, like in a competitive match, but there are restrictions making it often necessary for Mary to use the forehand overhead clear. For example, the feeder always plays shots high, to land between mid- and rear-court on Mary's side.

◯ Evaluation of workouts to develop skills

1. Judge whether the *intention* of the workout was clear. If you see a problem you should say what is wrong and be able to explain an appropriate alternative.

2. Judge whether an effective *assessment* of the performance of the skill was undertaken to identify areas of weakness. If you see a problem you should say what is wrong and be able to explain an appropriate alternative.

3. Judge whether the 'full marks' model was *taught/coached* effectively. If you see a problem you should say what is wrong and be able to explain an appropriate alternative.

4. Judge whether the *selection of practices* was appropriate for the situation. If you see a problem you should say what is wrong and be able to explain an appropriate alternative.

5. Judge whether the *organisation* was appropriate and effective. If you see a problem you should say what is wrong and be able to explain an appropriate alternative.

 ## TASK 1 on Workout for developing skills

Purpose

To develop your ability to plan safe, appropriate and effective workouts to develop skills.

To develop your ability to evaluate whether workouts are safe, appropriate and effective to develop skills.

Instructions

Plan and implement workouts to develop skills, using the principles and methods covered in this section. Get other students to evaluate your attempts and have them provide you with feedback.

Evaluate your fellow students' attempts to plan workouts to develop skills, and provide them with feedback.

 ## SUMMARY

In this section you have learnt the importance of:

- having a clear objective in planning a workout to develop skills
- using assessment tasks to identify areas of weakness in the performance of a selected skill
- teaching/coaching sound technique based on the 'full marks' model
- selecting appropriate practices for the skill and for the person's stage of learning
- organising the group and organising the time available

Conclusion

This book has provided you with the concepts, terminology, components, methods and principles needed to:

- plan exercise sessions and programmes to maintain good physical health/wellbeing
- plan training sessions and programmes to develop peak physical fitness for specific events and sports
- plan workouts to develop skilled performance in sports

You have also studied:

- how factors from lifestyle can influence health
- how to monitor, assess and evaluate the effectiveness of exercise and training programmes
- how health and safety issues need to be considered when exercising/training
- how genetic type factors can influence potential performance
- how other factors can influence participation in exercise and sport

©iStockphoto.com/ericsphotography

Over the course of your studies you should have developed your knowledge and thinking skills – for example, problem-solving, decision-making, planning and evaluating.

Take the information and skills you have learnt and be creative with them, but also be critical of what you do. You could be the person to discover a new or more effective way to train.

Finally, the book provides you with what you need to succeed in the GCSE examination. It also provides you with a sound foundation for further study at a higher level.